"I want to pray, but I d[...] said and heard this sai[...] out the years. In *The Se[...]* [...] the qualms, hesitations, and misunderstandings Christians have regarding prayer with biblical truth. Through witty and concise writing, Kyle makes the theology of prayer accessible to everyday life while stirring a deep desire in the reader to pray with humility. I cannot recommend this book enough!

Gretchen Saffles, author of *The Well-Watered Woman: Rooted in Truth, Growing in Grace, Flourishing in Faith* and founder of Well-Watered Women

Most of us struggle with prayer. I struggle with prayer. What's the secret to overcoming our struggles and learning to love prayer? In *The Secret to Prayer*, Kyle DiRoberts reminds us that it's simpler than we think. This practical, biblical, joyfully written book is a wonderful resource for anyone who struggles to pray. Read it over the course of a month. Read it with friends. Read it, and relax. Prayer shouldn't be a burden, but a blessing. This book will show you that.

Brett McCracken, senior editor, The Gospel Coalition and author of *The Wisdom Pyramid: Feeding Your Soul in a Post-Truth World* and *Uncomfortable: The Awkward and Essential Challenge of Christian Community*

This book is a wise, practical, insightful, biblically-based, and often delightful discussion of many dimensions of prayer that will certainly be helpful to everyone who reads it.

Wayne Grudem, distinguished research professor of Theology and Biblical Studies, Phoenix Seminary

Christians pray. That is not a controversial statement. But not all Christians practice prayer in the same way or understand it in the same manner. Kyle encourages people of faith to understand and practice prayer as an expression of love and humility in relationship with the sovereign of the universe. That God, who is fully and completely self-sufficient, would humble Himself to interact with His creatures is an amazing thought. And that thought really is what should drive our interaction with God in prayer. Using stories from his own life and others throughout history, Kyle draws the reader into the presence of God. This is an engaging book, written in a conversational style. The book models what it encourages the readers to adopt in their walk of faith and prayer.

Glenn R. Kreider, editor in chief, *Bibliotheca Sacra* and professor of Theological Studies, Dallas Theological Seminary

In *The Secret to Prayer*, Kyle DiRoberts offers keen insights into developing and truly enjoying prayer as a way of life. His reflections on God and our relationship to Him reveal prayer for what it is—a wonderful responsibility befitting a life changed by His grace. But make no mistake, this is not a detached academic manual about prayer but rather an invitation *to chase after a life of prayer*. With wit and relevance, DiRoberts helps us see anew how effective and essential this identity-shaping practice is at cultivating deeper fellowship with and affection for our triune God. Thankfully, some secrets are not meant to be kept.

Mark Yarbrough, president, Dallas Theological Seminary

If prayer seems like a secret language you haven't quite learned, then spend thirty-one days with Kyle DiRoberts as he decodes talking to God. Here is a kind and trustworthy teacher willing to open up his own prayer practices to show us why and how to take God up on His wild and wonderful invitation into conversation.

Lisa-Jo Baker, bestselling author of *Never Unfriended* and cohost of Out of the Ordinary

We have no substitutes for prayer, and there are no shortcuts. But for those of us who would like them, Kyle DiRoberts has written a wise and practical guide to the relational core of this spiritual foundation. For the distracted, the discouraged, the confused, and all us other stumbling misfits of prayer, this is a book of joyful medicine.

Paul J. Pastor, author of *The Face of the Deep*, *The Listening Day*, and *Bower Lodge*

Prayer—talking to and listening to God—is something that most people do, but also something most people have tons of anxiety about. This unease can plant seeds of confusion and doubt that grow into thorny weeds in your faith over time. With *The Secret to Prayer*, my friend Kyle welcomes you into an honest conversation where confusion is cleared up and important truths are shared. Incredibly approachable, this is an easy-to-read, quick-to-embrace book that you'll read and re-read, highlight and underline.

Jamie Rasmussen, senior pastor, Scottsdale Bible Church

THE

SECRET

TO

PRAYER

KYLE DIROBERTS

THE SECRET TO PRAYER

31 DAYS TO A MORE INTIMATE RELATIONSHIP WITH GOD

B&H
PUBLISHING
NASHVILLE, TENNESSEE

Published by B&H Publishing Group
Nashville, Tennessee

Dewey Decimal Classification: 248.3
Subject Heading: GOD / PRAYER / MEDITATIONS

Cover design by Micah Kandros; illustration by Softulka/
shutterstock. Author photo by Austin Kehmeier.

1 2 3 4 5 6 • 24 23 22 21

The secret of secrets:
humility is the soul of true prayer.
—ANDREW MURRAY

To Kaden, Oliver, and Carson

My first dream for this book was to write something for you boys. This is your book. Thank you for letting me share it with others too. May your humble hearts continue to grow toward the Lord. I love you.

To Lolly

You are my example of what is means to have a humble heart. I love you.

ACKNOWLEDGMENTS

Writing a book is a humbling experience. Why? Because no book worthy to be read was written alone. These are some of the people that helped me along the way.

Randy "Goz" Walters, thank you for taking the time to invest in me as a young kid trying to figure out what it means to have a relationship with God. Thank you for walking with me (literally!) toward Jesus on those hot summer days around the church and for introducing me to E. M. Bounds' work on prayer early on.

Bobby Brewer, thank you for always being there, always ready to pray for me with a simple, "I'm on it."

Wes Roberts, I am thankful for our time together each week. You have been a key source of encouragement through the years and have helped me discover and embrace God's calling upon my life. I know you and Judy pray for our family often.

Henry Holloman, I quickly realized in your class at TALBOT that you had been praying longer than I've been alive. You were first to introduce me to prayer not just as a spiritual discipline, but also as an academic pursuit. Also, thank you for being so humble and gracious to pass along your lecture notes on prayer to this young professor years later. I can only hope to carry on the tradition, and maybe, hand the notes over to another young professor one day.

Glenn Kreider, I miss not being able to grab poached eggs whenever we want. I miss not being able to stop by your office and trying to find a seat among all the books. But thanks for still making time for me, even from afar. Your writings on Jonathan Edwards and prayer helped shape so much of my thinking on this subject. You are my example of what it means to be a theologian. You and Jan have always been quick to pray for Lolly and I—for that we are thankful.

Paul Pastor, I'm sure it seemed like simple words of encouragement, but you actually pushed me along throughout the writing process. You have meant more than you know.

Susan Tjaden, I'm so thankful for your friendship. I always love when we get to talk and laugh. Thank you for always looking out for me. It was your suggestion that I include a discussion on unanswered prayer in this book.

Taylor Combs, thank you for believing in me. Let's be honest, it was the opening story about Justin Thomas and golf that had you. Throughout this process you have offered such wise counsel, and I couldn't have asked for a better editor and guide.

I want to thank my students, both new and old. Long before this book appeared on paper, it was with you that I would share through lectures and discussions, "The Secret to Prayer." You were the ones helping early on to sharpen my words.

I want to thank Scottsdale Bible Church for your encouragement and support. You shared Jesus with me when I was lost. Instilled the faith in me when I was young. And now have empowered me to exercise my spiritual gifts. I'm so thankful that I get to serve alongside the pastors at SBC.

Teresa Evenson, thank you for taking a chance on me. Having you by my side throughout this process has been an answer to prayer. I'm so thankful Susan introduced us. You get me and my writing. As an agent, you truly care about your authors and I'm thankful to be one of them. You are a great advocate and I've learned so much already just following your lead.

Mom and Dad, thank you for loving and encouraging me. No matter how crazy the dream is, your first response has never been "That's crazy!" or "No way!" Rather, your response has always been to help figure out how to make it a reality. I love you both so much.

Lolly, you are my favorite person. You are wise, smart, supportive, and beautiful. I would have never written this book without your encouragement. I still remember driving home from Show Low and you pushing me to finally embrace God's call to be an author. Your love for the Lord continues to encourage me and the boys more than you know. Thank you for loving me—I love you so much!

CONTENTS

Part III: Sin Makes You Holy

Part IV: Confess Your Sins to One Another

Part V: Keep Praying, God Isn't Annoyed

Part VI: Unanswered Prayer

INTRODUCTION

THE ILLNESS
OF PRAYER

My oldest son, Kaden, loves golf. And for only four years old, he's actually pretty good.

Proud dad speaking here. Or as my wife affectionately calls me, "Dance mom." Jokingly. *Lovingly.*

Kaden's two favorite players are Jordan Spieth and Justin Thomas.

Last year at the Waste Management Phoenix Open, Spieth and Thomas were paired together.

We were able to go to the tournament and, when we arrived, made our way to the tenth hole. From there, we planned to follow them for the rest of their round.

Kaden and I talk about these guys all the time. We *try* to recreate the shots we see them hit on TV. A lot of times we end up having more fun imitating their reactions to good shots and then adding a few moves of our own.

Typically, to win the Masters.

There was this moment out on the course at the Phoenix Open when Justin Thomas walked over and said hello to Kaden as we followed him down the fairway. Kaden froze.

He could not speak.

Thomas waved and asked Kaden if he was having fun.

Still no response.

Of course, after Thomas walked away, Kaden started talking again. He was amazed and confused as to why he couldn't speak. Inside he wanted to say something, but outside, he couldn't. Kaden kept asking if Thomas would come back so that he could try again.

Kaden's reaction captures how we often feel about prayer.

We've spoken about God with others.

We've heard some of the stories of the things He has done because someone prayed.

Maybe we've even heard people teach about prayer in a sermon or Bible study.

And then the moment arrives when it's time to talk to Him.

For everyone this moment is different. This is what makes each person's relationship with God so unique, and amazing, and beautiful, and without excuse, and terrifying. He has the ability to meet us right where we are.

But we all have this in common: we want to talk to God. We might not even know why we desire this so much, but we do. Even if we aren't entirely sure about how to pray or what to pray for, something in us desires His help. We might not even be too sure He exists, yet we still pray: "God, I don't know if You're real, but . . ."

So you seek Him, not as a spoiled child, demanding something from God. Rather, there is no one else you'd want to go to.

Then you pray, but questions and distractions flood your mind.

What do you mean, I'm talking to God?

Wait, can I talk to God about this? Are you sure?

You really think He cares about what I have to say or a need I have?

Do I talk to God like He's a friend or the Creator? Or both? How do you do that?

When I'm praying with someone else, I often get distracted because I'm listening to the words they say.

Why did they say it like that?

I never thought to say that.

Wait, am I still praying?

Is that okay to pray about that?

Is he preaching to me right now or praying?

It sounds like he's talking to me, but I thought he was talking to God.

I'm confused.

Or I get distracted because I'm watching people pray.

Yes, when a pastor says, "Bow your heads and close your eyes," I can't help but peek. It's so weird because I hear, "Pick your head up and open your eyes."

I remember feeling justified as a pastor, because then I had some kind of spiritual authority to look around during prayer. You know, in case someone raised their hand, I needed to be ready.

This book is about prayer. It's about all of that craziness I just shared that we all feel, to some degree, whenever we pray.

But this book is not about prayer as an action, as though it is something you do.

I'm not sure I care about that right now.

In other words, this book won't teach you words to repeat. It won't teach you how you should kneel. Or how you should hold your hands. Or which direction you should look.

How's my sales pitch so far? You excited to read this book?

Wait, don't answer that yet.

Imagine going to the doctor with a horrible cough. It has lingered for weeks. Finally, you make the appointment, show up twenty minutes early, fill everything out, and then wait because the doctor is running late.

I'm clearly not bitter.

You finally see the doctor, and she prescribes cough medicine. You go and purchase the cough medicine and begin immediately. But the cough doesn't go away.

So you go back to the same doctor. Her treatment plan is more of the same.

Wouldn't you stop going to that doctor? Perhaps see another doctor?

Why, though? Probably because you want someone to figure out why you are coughing and not just treat the symptom.

That's why I'm not going to discuss in detail the various methods of prayer, like what words to pray or the correct posture of prayer. Those are symptoms of prayer. Instead, I'd like to discuss a treatment plan that focuses on the illness, which is your heart. And my heart.

If we treat the heart, the symptoms will begin to take care of themselves over time. Maybe once the heart is aligned correctly, we'll settle into a new reality that God has given us great freedom in prayer. God has created us to pray, and our methods might look a little different or sound a little different than someone else's.

Maybe, for too long, we have been trying to get everyone to pray in a particular way (whatever that is) as if God only responds to certain types of prayers, so we conform our actions in prayer to mirror someone else's. Yet all along, God has cared more about the heart that was producing the prayers than He did about the mechanics employed.

So what's the treatment plan?

Humility.

Not just any dose of humility.

A humble heart.

Let me explain what that means. A humble heart is like a child who just wants her mom or dad and doesn't care what it takes to get their attention. Little children don't care if you are talking to someone else; interrupting you isn't a problem. They don't care if they have asked fifteen times; they'll probably ask another fifteen times. They don't care if the question makes sense; they assume you'll figure it out. They don't care if you've said no; they just ask again and again and again.

It's one thing for a child to talk to a parent this way, but it's a whole different story when an adult behaves like a child. No matter how old, wise, or experienced you are, a humble heart always maintains this childlike posture before the Lord.

This book explores prayer long before it ever forms into a group of words. Long before it unlocks all the things we desire or want from God. Long before we think about praying.

What does prayer look like?

Well, I don't know.

I can visibly see you with your eyes closed, seemingly talking to someone else. I can hear you talking to God and the words you are speaking to Him. Yet it's the heart that is the wordsmith, working diligently from within to produce the words spoken to God. God hears the words you pray because He hears your heart.

This presents a great difficulty for us when it comes to prayer, because it is really hard for us to know with certainty the content of our own heart.

In other words, we say the words. We hear the words, but we don't always *know* if our hearts are humble.

It's scary. I can produce good words from an evil heart. I can fool you, make you think I'm praying this super spiritual prayer, maybe even make you jealous of the prayer I just prayed, and yet have the worst of intentions.

What's also scary is that I can produce an awful-sounding prayer, maybe even sound like I don't know what I'm doing (maybe I don't!), mix up and mess up words all over, but these words I'm attempting to string together in prayer are coming from a humble heart.

Can you guess who most Christians would model their prayers after?

What about who God would recommend we mimic?

Once we begin to dwell upon the kind of heart we have, the intimate prayer life we've longed for will appear. I don't mean magically appear. But it will come to life. Words from a humble heart flow like a rushing river. We will experience great freedom because we will realize that all along God does not care about the words so much as He cares about the heart producing the words.

My fear is that people have been teaching you merely the mechanics of prayer all this time, or maybe these are the only types of questions you've been asking. This isn't necessarily wrong, especially when we have a long history of prayer in the church. People have written extensively about how great men and women from many different Christian traditions have prayed.

> God does not care about the words so much as He cares about the heart producing the words.

You might have achieved what you perceive to be success in prayer because God answered you. I hope that by the end of this book, you will measure success a little differently. Perhaps success in prayer is measured not by God answering our prayers, but by our ability to know if the prayers produced are from a humble heart, regardless of the answer.

Pursuing a humble heart has the potential to affect many areas in your life, not just prayer. You might be thinking, "That's great! I'd love that." But we can't avoid that we, as Americans, pride ourselves (see what I did there?) in our own abilities. If you give America a bunch of steel, we build towers and bridges and walls. We find all the natural resources in our country so that we can be self-sufficient. We build a military that the world fears so that we never have to worry, and maybe we even force other countries and leaders to rely on us in times of need.

Individually, we strive for the American dream, which means we never have to rely on someone else. If you've "made it," that means your family doesn't have to worry about money, food, shelter, or clothing. You are able to provide these things by yourself.

But this attitude won't work when you try to pray. I'm going to try to persuade you to believe that what's most important when you pray is that your heart is humble before the Lord, that you are dependent on God for everything, and that you are never spiritually self-sufficient. Instead, you are poor, hungry, desperate, naked, and in need of help.

This book contends that somewhere between the humble heart of man and God resides the beauty, mystery, conversation, and intimacy we so desperately desire in prayer.

If I'm honest, looking inward at the heart can be really scary stuff because of what it might reveal.

It's okay, I'm not going to leave you throughout this adventure. There are no shortcuts. We won't be able to go around it or over it; we're going to have to go through it. Together. And I've seen my heart (still looking, actually), and I won't have any room to judge along the way.

PART I
THEO-TALK

There can be no substitute for prayer. Here we speak not merely of times set apart when we fold hands and bow heads, but also of a way of being.
—KELLY KAPIC

INTRODUCTION
TO PART I

How do we pray from a humble heart?

Good question.

It's hard.

It would be far easier to write about what humble prayers sound like or look like because, then, they could be copied or adapted by each person. But correct words are not necessarily indicators of a humble heart. That just means you know how to sound humble. Proper posture does not indicate a humble heart either. It simply means you know how to look the part.

In order to embrace a humble heart in prayer, we have to believe some specific theological truths about God. That's what we are going to explore in this part of the book.

Unfortunately, I can't present humility in a systematized way. Humility isn't that easy. Humility isn't that structured. It's more of an art.

I'd rather us envision these humble truths about the divine–human relationship in prayer as a mosaic, with the hope that in the end we will see individually and collectively something beautiful.

As this part of the book ("Theo-Talk") draws upon God's conversational relationship with us, an important relationship of mine continues to resurface over and over again. Unique to "Theo-Talk" are various stories about my two boys. Hidden in them are images of some of the ways we comprehend our relationship with God. In a way, my sons pray to me all the time.

CHAPTER 1

SWING YOUR SWING

Human beings are created in the image of God (*imago dei*), which means you are not just something, but someone.

A unique someone.

With a unique language.

Our mind, our emotions, our heritage, our experiences all help shape who we are long before the words we choose to speak take form.

It would be boring if we all expressed ourselves the same way.

The beauty (and difficulty) of a relationship is that we have to know who we are talking to if we really want to understand what the other person is saying. The words we choose to employ in a conversation could be the same words another might use, but what sets words apart is that they come from a certain person with a unique personality, heart, and mind.

Dictionaries are helpful in that they provide the meaning of a word, but dictionaries are useless when it comes to understanding the person using those words.

To have a relationship with another person is a humbling experience, because each person can't participate in that relationship with the assumption that he or she knows everything. Or even a little. The pitfall of assumptions is that the one assuming is self-reliant in the relationship and not dependent on the other person.

It is also difficult to maintain a relationship with a person who thinks he or she knows everything. To be a friend, one must observe, listen, be present, and ask questions.

When you first meet someone, you have no shared vocabulary. Even when you're on friendly terms, you might not grasp the meaning of his or her words because you haven't spent the time or effort to get to know him or her. Once you begin to understand another person, his or her words begin to make more sense. In other words, the more I get to know someone, the more he or she makes sense to me.

This means we need to listen to our friends, family, and neighbors as though we have never heard the words they're speaking before. Because we haven't, and who knows if we will ever hear them spoken like that again?

God knows us this way.

He not only knows the words we are choosing to communicate, He also knows the experiences causing us to choose those specific words. God celebrates our uniqueness, yet often in prayer, we desire to fit in to some common mold as if there is just one way to pray. It's as though we think we have to have a prayer language that is totally different from how we speak to anyone else.

At first glance, this makes sense. In prayer, we aren't talking to just anyone. We are talking to *God*.

But what if our prayer language came from the same words we speak on a daily basis?

The same words we speak to our children. Our spouse. Our friends. Our coworkers. Our baristas. Our . . .

What if it isn't necessary to use a whole new set of words that we only use when we speak to God?

Instead, why not use the words we are most familiar with? If I'm honest, if you really want me to "pray constantly" (1 Thess. 5:17), it would be much easier for me to attempt this if I could just use the words I speak most often.

Part of what makes prayer so uncomfortable is that we are so accustomed to speaking to our friends without any concern about the content of our heart. Then, in prayer, it's hard to make the transition to communicating to God, even to the point that something doesn't feel right as we speak to God.

I wonder if that discomfort is due to a heartfelt reality that we know we can't speak to God with the same words we use when speaking to others.

Maybe we avoid the internal dilemma, and we just dodge speaking to God altogether. Or we get creative, and we speak to God with humble words but from a prideful heart.

So what do we do? Maybe we need to address the root of the problem and not the symptom. Maybe we need to treat the illness rather than the cough. Maybe we need God to change our hearts.

Psalm 139 describes what God knows about you.

He knows when you sit down. When you stand up. When you lie down. Thoughts before you think them. All this led the psalmist to proclaim: "I have been remarkably and wondrously made" (Ps. 139:14).

The psalmist did add one other aspect of God's knowledge: "Before a word is on my tongue, you know all about it, LORD" (Ps. 139:4).

This means there is diversity and creativity in the way you and I speak to God. He knows my words, your words, her words, his words. God knows our words altogether. Even though we all speak different words. That is what amazed the psalmist—that God would have that kind of knowledge about us.

Moreover, in Psalm 139, God's knowledge is such that He knows thoughts before we speak them. This is beautiful on a number of levels, but one reason is that God knows our personalities, experiences, presuppositions, and biases long before we get to the point of speaking.

Jesus picked up on this in the stories we read about Him in the Gospels. He didn't praise someone for the words they spoke and then model those words over and over again to the disciples, as if the words were the rubric to effective prayer. Rather, he puts before us a diverse range of individuals to learn from—like a widow, a tax collector, a fishermen, and a doctor. What is common to them all? They have a humble heart.

> God receives prayer from a humble heart.

God receives prayer from a humble heart.

If God creates us in His image, and that image is reflected in the diverse and different words humans speak, then His ability to understand us must be matched by His ability to understand the personalities and experiences that produce those words.

How many people refrain from praying because they don't have the perfect words put together in their mind?

Or how many hold off on praying because they don't sound as "put together" as someone else?

These are bad reasons not to pray.

God is fully capable of walking with us and absorbing our prayers whether we are new Christians or have been praying for a century.

One of my favorite golfers is Arnold Palmer. (I promise this is my last golf story.) You may be more familiar with his signature logo: the rainbow-colored umbrella. Or maybe his famous drink, which was half lemonade, half iced tea. But he is most famous for injecting the game of golf into pop culture.

Arnie made it cool to be a golfer.

There is a quote from Palmer, and if you have the time, go look it up; it's even cooler *hearing* him say it.

Palmer says this:

> Swing your swing. Not some idea of a swing. Not a swing you saw on TV. Not that swing you wish you had. No, swing your swing. Capable of greatness. Prized only by you. Perfect in its imperfection. Swing your swing. I know, I did.[1]

And he did. He had a very unique swing.

I love this quote, and I often think of prayer when I read it.

> Don't pray like me.
> Or your friend.

---

[1] https://golf.com/instruction/arnold-palmer-quote-swing-your-swing/

Or your pastor.

Or your favorite theologian.

Or anyone else for that matter.

Your humble prayers are perfect in their imperfections. Speak your language, pray *your* prayer, from a humble heart.

CHAPTER 2

NAKED

R ight from the start, so that there isn't any confusion, the
Bible describes that God is the Creator.

Of everything.

"In the beginning God created the heavens and the earth"
(Gen. 1:1).

Day and night, land and sea, and everything that inhabits
the earth. Including all the living creatures. God created it all.

However, toward the end of creation He brings forth
something different, something in God's image. After His
likeness. Humans. Both male and female were created, *equally.*

Genesis 1:27 says: "So God created man in his own image;
he created him in the image of God; *he created them male and
female.*"

Prior to the creation of humans, God told the living creatures
to be fruitful and multiply, and they listened and obeyed their
Creator. He said the same thing to Adam and Eve; however,
that's not all He said.

God also gave them the keys to His creation. He told them about His creation and how to use it. And not just use it, but enjoy it.

Adam and Eve were to care for and find pleasure in God's new creation. This meant they were to preserve it. Recycle. Reduce pollution. Travel. Create. That kind of stuff.

After God declared that His creation was very good in Genesis 1, He rested, and then the Bible circles back to a more detailed discussion about the creation of man and woman in Genesis 2.

It is worth remembering that God had already created male and female in chapter 1. In chapter 2, we find out a little more. And this reveals a conversation between God and Adam.

We don't know a lot about this conversation, but we do know that God brought each living creature to Adam so that he could name them. Together they accomplished this work. Adam was created with the capacity to speak to God and to accomplish this work together with God.

Even though Adam had a relationship with God, God said that it wasn't good for Adam to be alone. Even in the midst of being with God, there was still something missing.

Often it is said that Adam was not complete until he got married.

Not necessarily.

God recognized that it was not good for Adam to be alone. But why? The answer had to do with Adam being created in God's image.

As Christians, we believe that God is one being, eternally existent as three persons. Theologically, we call this the doctrine of the trinity. For our purposes, it goes like this: Adam was created by God, who is one being, eternally existent as three persons (Father, Son, and Holy Spirit). Because he was created in the image of God, who lives in triune community, Adam's nature cried out for community.

Adam's nature didn't cry out for marriage. The helper God created for Adam was not simply to elevate marriage; rather, it was to say that if God creates something in His image, that something isn't meant to be alone. You aren't meant to be alone.

Adam's relational deficiency was not defined by an inability to speak to someone, or live in the presence of someone. He was talking with God, and together they named the animals. However, Adam did lack an equal companion. So God created a partner suitable for him. Equal to him.

To live in community together.

Yes, Adam and Eve did get married, and they became one flesh.

You've probably heard this described during a marriage ceremony before, when the pastor often quotes Genesis 2:24: "This is why a man leaves his father and mother and bonds with his wife, and they become one flesh." Somehow, supernaturally, Adam and Eve remained two persons, and yet, spiritually speaking, they became one.

This defies mathematics, but it works theologically. Actually, come to think of it, theologians make for awful mathematicians.

Take God, for example. Christians believe that God is one being (or nature), eternally existent as three persons. Somehow, $1 = 3$ works in the Trinity.

Or take Jesus. Christians affirm this doctrine called the hypostatic union, which affirms that Jesus is one person with two natures. A fully divine nature and a fully human nature. Somehow, 2 = 1 works with Christ.

Okay, back to the garden.

After the Bible describes Adam and Eve as becoming one flesh, the Bible then describes Adam and Eve as being naked—in their birthday suits.

But what is crazy is they were naked and *not ashamed.*

Genesis 2:25 says: "Both the man and his wife were naked, yet felt no shame."

They were naked and felt no hesitation, no remorse, no guilt, no humiliation, no disappointment, no discomfort, no shame.

Sin was about to enter the world, but let's pause and rest and realize that all is well for a moment. God's creation was finished. It was very good. God was able to live in community with all His creation, and yet there was this unique humankind of creation, made in His image, with which He was able to converse. All was right in the relationship of humans to one another—they were naked and felt no shame. All was right in the relationship of humans to the created world. And all was right in the relationship of humans to God.

CHAPTER 3

CLOTHED

Speaking to one another in the garden of Eden was quite normal. Adam and Eve not only could talk to each other, but they could also converse with God. Eve was even able to speak to the serpent—which makes me wonder if they could speak to the other animals too. And if that's the case, do you think any of the animals had reactions to what Adam named them? Can you imagine some animal walking with his head down, looking defeated, and Eve says, "What's wrong?" The animal looks up at Eve gloomily. "He named me *elephant*. I'm an elephant?!" I don't know about you, but I'm hopeful that when we're in heaven, we'll be able to speak to animals again.

Have you ever wondered why speaking to the serpent wasn't admonished as sinful?

If anything, it seems like Eve was pretty comfortable around the serpent. It's as though they'd had many conversations in the past. One might even say that she was friendly, not only with a sinner, but the one who helped bring sin into the world!

I have this friend named Susan. She is not a serpent, nor did she bring sin into the world. She is one of those friends that God brings into your life as a gift, right before life gets bad. We don't get to talk as much as we'd like, but when we do, we tell stories and laugh a lot.

In a past life she was a geological scientist who tracked earthquakes. Now she is an editor for a big publishing house. Totally makes sense, right?

Susan has these great stories about going to the site of a recent earthquake and measuring the earth, trying to find the exact place where the earthquake occurred. Then she would record all the data from the aftershocks.

Through the course of our conversations, I learned about a new term: *tectonic plates*. Tectonic plates exist under the earth's surface. When these plates shift or move beneath the earth, it causes an earthquake.

As she described these tectonic plates shifting, I couldn't help but think of another kind of earthquake—a spiritual earthquake, when something so significant happens that it's as though the tectonic plates of life shift, causing the world around us to shake.

As though to say, the world will never be the same.

The Bible contains earthquakes: stories like the Flood, the Exodus, the birth of Jesus, the death of Jesus, and the resurrection of Jesus.

And by the way, Christians are anticipating another earthquake—a *big* one—when Jesus returns.

In Genesis 3:6–10, the tectonic plates of the divine–human relationship shifted, causing a massive earthquake. It reads:

The woman saw that the tree was good for food
and delightful to look at, and that it was desirable for obtaining wisdom. So she took some of
its fruit and ate it; she also gave some to her
husband, who was with her, and he ate it. Then
the eyes of both of them were opened, and they
knew they were naked; so they sewed fig leaves
together and made coverings for themselves.

Then the man and his wife heard the sound
of the LORD God walking in the garden at the
time of the evening breeze, and they hid from
the LORD God among the trees of the garden.
So the LORD God called out to the man and said
to him, "Where are you?"

And he said, "I heard you in the garden,
and I was afraid because I was naked, so I hid."

There it is. The relational tectonic plates between God and
humans shifted due to sin. Things would never be the same.

Notice that once Adam and Eve sinned, they didn't immediately
die. However, the humbling process of death began as they
experienced physical, spiritual,
and emotional brokenness for
the first time.

Notice how the Bible
describes that when Adam and
Eve heard the Lord walking in
the garden, they hid themselves
from Him. No words were
spoken; they simply heard the
sound of the Lord walking, and

> In Genesis 3:6–10,
> the tectonic plates
> of the divine–human
> relationship shifted,
> causing a massive
> earthquake.

they hid (Gen. 3:8). Then the Lord called for Adam and Eve: "Where are you?" What do they say from their hiding place? "I heard you in the garden, and *I was afraid* because I was naked, so I hid" (Gen. 3:10, emphasis mine).

Their relational response to God after the Fall was to be afraid of Him—to feel shame simply being in His presence.

God asked Adam how this happened, and Adam, like a real man, blamed Eve.

And Eve blamed the serpent.

Then the Lord rebuked the serpent.

Then Eve.

Then Adam.

After this earthquake, a new reality set in. Humanity's relationship with God was going to have to be different going forward.

The moment when Adam and Eve became afraid and ashamed is interesting. It wasn't after the Lord rebuked them. Instead, they felt shame long before the rebuking.

Shame is different than guilt.

Guilt awakens a person, which can lead him or her to repentance. Guilt helps a person recognize wrongdoing. Guilt convinces a person he or she has done something wrong. Guilt is humbling because it exposes a person's weaknesses. Guilt makes it really difficult to sell the false face of perfection.

Shame, on the other hand, leads one away from God. Shame takes the humbling effects of guilt and says, "You're embarrassing to God. You humiliate God. God is sorry He has a relationship with you."

God did not shame Adam and Eve. He does not shame you either.

The tectonic plates shifted, causing a massive relational earthquake, yet Adam and Eve were still able to speak to God. God was still able to hear Adam and Eve. And God was able to provide for their needs. God is gracious.

God is gracious? Follow me on this.

At the very end of this narrative God sent them out from the garden of Eden, but not without first extending grace to them. How did He give them grace? He clothed them.

The Bible says: "The LORD God made clothing from skins for the man and his wife, and he *clothed* them" (Gen. 3:21).

There is a Greek version of the Old Testament called the Septuagint. It was created by Greek-speaking Jews in Alexandria around the middle of the third century. Biblical scholars appreciate this translation because it provides a window into the Second Temple time period as well as an understanding of how certain words were understood.

This particular translation of the Bible is helpful to us here. In Genesis 3:21 in the Septuagint, the Greek word for "clothed" is *enedusen*. This is the same word used elsewhere in the New Testament to talk about Christians who have "put on" or clothed themselves with Christ.

For example, Galatians 3:27 says: "For those of you who were baptized into Christ have been *enedusen* with Christ." In other words, Paul is saying that as Christians believe in the Lord Jesus and are saved, they are baptized in Christ; in other words, they clothe themselves with Christ.

After the Fall, and before He removed Adam and Eve from the garden, God called them to Himself, and He clothed them.

But weren't Adam and Eve already clothed?

Yep.

Remember, they sewed fig leaves together and made clothes for themselves (Gen. 3:7). But, for God, this wasn't good enough. Not for His creation. The way they managed to clothe themselves wasn't good enough for the One who created them.

God, even after the Fall, even though He was about to remove them from the garden, wanted to graciously clothe them.

So He did.

Almost as soon as God introduced humans into the biblical narrative, He also introduced grace.

What's so amazing about grace? That God will clothe them again later. With Himself.

CHAPTER 4

AWKWARD

A s a loving and supportive husband, one of my duties when Lolly and I are at dinner together or running errands is to make her feel awkward.

Do you know this feeling? Where all you want to do is be somewhere else? Or maybe you think it'd just be better if you disappeared.

For Lolly this typically happens when I randomly talk to people or tell a joke, thinking it will be received with laughter, only to discover the person has no sense of humor and takes me far too seriously.

It typically goes like this: Someone trips right next to us, and I'll say something like, "Oh, watch your step. Glad you're okay. I almost thought we lost you there."

Typically, they stare, I laugh, and Lolly looks down or walks away feeling so *awkward*.

This = Success.

Life is filled with awkward conversations. Marriage alone provides enough of them.

Remember the dreaded DTR? Define. The. Relationship. Is this still a thing? Do people still have this conversation?

Lolly and I were eating at an old favorite restaurant of ours called Delux when ours happened. I'm using "happened" loosely here, because I'm not sure it simply happened; I'm pretty sure Lolly preordained it to be.

This was back in the mid-2000s and the Phoenix Suns were playing amazing basketball. Shawn Marion, Steve Nash, Amar'e Stoudemire, Leandro Barbosa, and the dreaded Spurs. I was completely sucked in, watching as many minutes of as many games as I could. And Lolly had had enough. She basically said, "Pick me or the Suns."

Well, I made my decision. The Suns totally understood, and the rest is history.

Even after all these years of marriage, Lolly and I still have awkward conversations. Awkward conversations are necessary. They reveal that you really love the person. They demonstrate to the one you love that you'll pursue them at all costs. Even when it isn't comfortable.

No one told me that before I got married. Any time two inherently flawed people embark on a relationship, be prepared for awkward.

Trust me, there are times when it would be far easier for Lolly and I to avoid the awkward and just move on.

Remember when your parents or grandparents talked about not letting the sun go down on your anger? Did you know that is a Bible verse? "Don't let the sun go down on your anger" (Eph. 4:26). See, I told you.

Even though this verse isn't in reference to marriage, it applies to it. But this verse doesn't support the idea that in order to prevent anger, just avoid fighting. Nor does this verse mean we should pretend that we don't fight. This verse means that we should talk with one another—especially when we've sinned against one another.

This also means we need to have *that* awkward conversation, and we need to have that conversation soon, because the sun is setting.

Isn't it interesting that the "timer" to have this conversation is the sun? Thankfully, from our perspective, it moves slowly, but it never stops and eventually goes away for the night. It's like the verse is saying, "You can go ahead and be mad or grumpy all you want. You can procrastinate and stall. But that sun is heading west. And there is no reason you can't settle down, find some courage, and talk before it disappears."

Prayer is awkward too, and I think the sooner you embrace it, the more you'll pray. More frequently, freely, honestly, and humbly.

So what is so awkward about prayer?

Honestly, I think it's the same with any other conversation. I participate in it as a sinner. What's different, though, is that God's perfect. When two humans talk to one another, they do so as sinners. When a creature talks to their Creator, the creature does so as a sinner, talking to God, who is perfect.

Right from the start, sin makes prayer tricky. It causes us to constantly question our motives in prayer. For example, when God responds to our prayer, sin makes it really difficult for us to recognize God's revelation and answer to our prayer. If, due to sin, we have a hard time grasping God's answer to our

Sin makes prayer tricky.

prayer, we begin to think God doesn't care. Or doesn't listen. Or maybe we aren't saying the right words.

Unfortunately, because our very nature is sinful, we will always experience tension and discomfort as we pray to God.

In some weird way, one of my objectives of this book is to get us to realize that tension and discomfort are natural. And as long as our sinful nature affects us—spiritually, mentally, physically, emotionally—it makes prayer feel very *un*natural.

That's the dirty little secret.

Sin does not merely have heaven and hell consequences, but it also affects our relationship with God here and now, specifically regarding the comfort and ease we long to have when we pray.

What if there is divine purpose in the awkwardness of prayer? What if prayer was designed to keep us balanced in this strange tension? One that says we are welcome to pray often, about anything, without ceasing, and with persistence. Yet we will never feel fully comfortable because of our nature and the nature of the One to whom we are speaking.

> If you are waiting until you feel comfortable in prayer, you might never begin praying.

In other words, if you are waiting until you feel comfortable in prayer, you might never begin praying.

This intimidates Christians. It frustrates us, confuses us, and silences us.

Sin has deeply, totally impacted our nature, making praying hard enough. Then, there is the whole waiting, watching, and listening for the Lord's response. Sadly, the reaction to this intimidation is often that we refrain from praying.

I want to change this response. By the end of this book, I hope we will have begun to change.

But for the moment, I need us to at least acknowledge that prayer is awkward. And that's okay, because praying to a perfect, omniscient (all-knowing), omnisapient (all-wise), invisible, omnibenevolent (infinitely good), omnipotent (all-powerful), sovereign God takes some getting used to.

And maybe you'll never fully get used to that.

Maybe you aren't supposed to fully get used to that.

Maybe this reality is what keeps us *humble* as we pray—which is right where we need to be.

CHAPTER 5

FAITH

Yes, conversations can be awkward, but that's okay. Remember?

Please say yes, because it was *just* the last chapter.

Awkwardness in prayer is not just okay, it may even be essential to beginning and maintaining a conversational relationship with God.

In prayer, the term *conversation* is a word worth thinking about. Here's why.

When you and I talk to each other, we share words with one another. Either on the phone, through text—or even now through emojis and gifs. Then we speak without even uttering a word. With our body language and mannerisms, we can communicate all kinds of things.

But what does it mean to have a conversation with God? Is talking to God similar to when I talk to my closest friend? Christians sometimes refer to God as "Abba, Father," so does that mean I talk to God like I talk to my earthly father?

I don't think so.

When having a conversation with God, it's not typical for God to speak back. In fact, in prayer you might never hear God speak back to you in an audible voice.

I think this might not even be the way God designed prayer.

Instead, when we think of having a conversation with God, we are using our words in order to communicate to God, but God does not use our words to communicate back.

But what about the Bible? Didn't God use human words in order to communicate His truth to us in the Bible?

Yes, He did.

But remember, we are talking about prayer, not reading the Bible.

I'm assuming that in prayer you are asking God questions about life. Perhaps seeking wisdom, like which job you should take, whom you should marry, where you should move. I bet you have prayed and asked God questions that, if He were to answer, He'd have to reveal His response to you in some other way because there isn't a verse in the Bible that addresses specifically what you are asking.

What do you do then?

The answer to *this* question is what I am speaking to.

Prayer is communication from man to God, and not from God to man. This sounds like a weird conversation to have, right? In fact, can we even call it a conversation?

We've all had those "conversations" with that person who loves to talk. Even if you try, you can't get a word in edgewise. So what do we do? We avoid them.

Yet here I am trying to get you to adopt this person's communication habits in prayer, where you talk and talk and talk, and God never responds audibly. *But no one wants to talk to this person*, you're thinking. *If I don't want to talk to this person, why would God want to listen to this person?*

What if the term *conversation*, as it relates to God, means something different from when you and I describe our interactions with each other?

In theology, we do this all the time. We use one word, but we understand it to have multiple meanings—which makes sense when you think about how limited we are. We, limited beings, are using human language to try to describe a God who is quite indescribable.

Take, for example, the word *person*. As Christians, when we talk about the Trinitarian God, what we mean is that God is one *being*, eternally existent as three *persons*: the Father, the Son, and the Holy Spirit.

However, when we talk about Jesus Christ, we understand that Jesus is one *person*, with two *natures*: fully God, fully human.

Thus, for a Christian, when we speak of God's *personhood*, we might be referencing one or three. Both of which we confess to be theologically true statements about the word *person*.

When a Christian speaks of God's nature, we might be referencing one (in reference to the Trinity) or two (in reference to the two natures of Jesus). Both of these we confess to be true theologically about the word *nature*.

The term *conversation* is no different.

When we use the term *conversation* to describe our interaction with one another, that doesn't mean the term must be applied to God so that He has a conversation with us just like we have a conversation with our friends. Instead, God's response to our prayer is found in His revelation to us. That means God's response to our prayer will not look like, or sound like, how we respond to each other.

God's response to me in prayer might look different from His response to you. And He knows you so well that He knows how to respond best to you.

Maybe you tried to pray a long time ago, and you never heard from God. By "heard," I mean you were literally expecting to hear something from God. You never heard the audible voice of God, never heard even the quiet voice of God from within— but does that mean God ignored your prayer?

Maybe He revealed His answer to your prayer, and you missed it because you were expecting something different.

In prayer, we speak to God, and He reveals to us. This is how the conversation works.

Let's keep going.

If God's response to our prayer is His revelation, the one praying must remain in a constant position to receive. This is a humbling posture, which is exactly where God wants us.

It would be far easier if we knew how and when God was going to respond. If this were the case, we could go about our days with little attention given to God because we would possess the confidence to know what it will be like when He reveals His answer.

But we don't. Instead, we just wait and wonder, and we can't get too distracted, because we might miss Him. Prayer is a humbling experience as we wait for God to disclose Himself, to unveil His answer.

This means we must be dependent on our faith that God is good, that He is the giver and responder, and we won't know what He has given until He reveals it to us.

Remember Thomas? You know, doubting Thomas.

I actually think people are too hard on him. I like him. Probably because I can relate to him.

Thomas wouldn't believe until he was able to see (or touch) Jesus' scars in both His hands and side. Do you remember how Jesus responded to Thomas? "Oh, Thomas (probably), blessed are those who believe but do not see."

We'll get to the phrase "Blessed are those who have not seen and yet believe" in a moment, but before that, we have to let God's grace settle in. Before Jesus declared that faith is evident when we believe without seeing, Jesus *still* stretched His arms out and let Thomas touch where the nails pierced. Then He let Thomas touch His side (John 20:27).

The command is to believe without seeing, and Jesus meant it.

But Jesus also helps Thomas in his weakness.

I'm thankful Jesus responded this way, because there are times (many times) when I know the right answer, but I can't embody it. I can't accept it. I can't trust it. What Jesus has shown me through His interaction with Thomas is that He will still be gracious with me as I'm learning what it means to live by faith.

Prayer is similar. It takes faith to believe that God will respond to our prayer.

It may take time for God to reveal His response to our prayer. Time takes faith. And His response may be different than we hoped for or expected.

What do we do when we think God might have revealed Himself and answered our prayer?

A good place to start would be comparing what we *think* God might be saying to what we *know* God *has said* to us in His

Word. This dependency on the Word of God helps us to develop confidence as we seek answers to our prayers.

A warning, though, as we interpret what God has revealed: remember the tectonic plates Susan taught us about? The ones that shifted when sin entered the world? How it changed everything, including our relationship with God?

One of the side effects of this shift is the way it complicates our conversations with God, because now when we interpret His revelation, we can't forget that our sin nature desires to work against us and inhibit our ability to interpret what God has revealed.

Thus, your interpretation might be wrong.

In other words, the desire of Satan is to make you think God has revealed Himself when He hasn't. This means we must be humble enough to expect that our interpretation of what we perceive to be an answer to our prayer might be subject to error because we are sinners trying to understand and interpret God's revelation.

The big picture of prayer is humbling enough, because the very idea that we have to go to someone else for help demonstrates our insufficiencies. And if you pray a lot, you are aware of your insufficiencies a lot.

Then, we have no idea how God is going to respond to our prayer, which is also humbling because we have to live in a waiting, observant posture.

Prayer is pretty much a lot of waiting, and watching, and observing, and being wrong, and waiting some more, until God finally discloses Himself through the means that He so chooses.

This conversation works as long as you are humble.

A humble heart doesn't have a problem being wrong, doesn't have a problem waiting, doesn't attempt to manufacture something to declare as God's revelation, and doesn't have a problem trusting.

A humble heart faithfully, persistently, and watchfully seeks God in prayer.

CHAPTER 6

EVERYTHING

God knows everything.

There is a theological word to describe this attribute of God: *omniscience*.

If God wasn't omniscient, how could He be God? If He didn't know everything, why would you want to pray to Him?

When we make the claim that God knows everything, this means that God knows Himself and all that could be, would be, and will be.

Psalm 139 tells us about the kind of knowledge God has about us. God knows when we will sit down or stand up. Our thoughts before we think them. Our words before we speak them. Our prayers before we pray them. And the accompanying circumstances and needs that brought about the prayer.

Yet God knows all these things in one eternal moment.

Think about this for a second (or maybe the rest of the day).

God knows all the times in your life that you will pray. You don't know all the times you will pray. Instead, you come to know each time you pray as you pray.

In other words, your knowledge of how much you have prayed only goes so far as the last time you have prayed. It's only at the end of your life that you could be able to know all the times you have prayed.

Yet it's something that God has always known.

That's why, whenever you are presented with the opportunity to pray or not to pray, you should always choose to pray, and come to know yet another moment in which you have prayed—a moment God has always known about.

If this kind of knowledge isn't impressive enough, we learn in Psalm 139:16 that this knowledge God has about us predates our birth, when we were an unformed substance.

An unformed what?

Yes, substance.

What is a substance?

I'm not sure.

Psalm 139:16 (esv) says, "Your eyes saw my *unformed substance*; in your book were written, every one of them, the days that were formed for me, when as yet there was none of them."

This verse is saying something amazing about what exactly God knows. The Hebrew word for "unformed substance" is *golm*, and the only occurrence in the Bible is found in this verse. At the very least, it means something like an embryo in a mother's womb.

God's intimate knowledge concerning His children is such that He knows when we will sit down or stand up, our thoughts before we think them, our words before we speak them, and our prayers before we pray them—all before we are born. It wasn't as though God was looking upon an already created you and waiting and watching so that He could know when you would speak or sit down or think or pray.

No, you were just a formless substance.

I can really relate to this. Well, as far as my kids are concerned. They think I know *everything*.

As far as Lolly is concerned . . .

Even if I don't know the answer, coming up with something isn't too difficult.

Even with this kind of knowledge I possess, never once as a father have I thought to myself that talking to my kids is boring or a waste of time because I already know the answer. When they come running up to me and I know exactly what they are going to ask, I don't stop them before they say a word and give them an answer. No way! I listen to them and watch their facial expressions and pay attention and enjoy every word that comes out of their mouths. Oliver, in particular, has this adorable pirate face he's been working on lately when he asks for something. He squints one eye, lifts his lip like Elvis, and turns his head to the side. . . . How can you say no?

I know what candy they want, what movie they want to watch, what food they want to eat. And yet, it never gets old.

So much so, that Lolly and I are begging them to never grow up.

Also, you would have to ask Kaden and Oliver, but I don't think they've ever felt a relational facade because they are talking to their dad, who knows everything.

(Um, if you do end up asking Kaden and Oliver if they feel that way, you'll probably have to define *facade* for them.)

If anything, it seems like they love talking to me for that very reason. Oliver is still a bit too young, but Kaden loves to ask questions about all kinds of things, especially about sports. "Daddy, what's a strikeout? Daddy, how do you know how many outs there are? Daddy, why do you like Derek Jeter so much? Daddy, do I have to like the Yankees too?" Without fail, Kaden will always ask, "Daddy, why do you know *everything* about baseball?"

He loves to ask questions, and I love to answer his questions.

One of the special ways Oliver and Kaden know I'm present and available is if I'm willing to entertain and answer their questions. They feel bonded to me because my attention is theirs, and once they know this they don't stop asking.

It's weird, though. I hear these stories from parents with kids who are much older than mine. They tell me that one day my kids will grow up and not care about anything that I know. In fact, they will tell me that I *don't* know anything. And whatever it is that I *think* I know is, in fact, wrong and that I should know better.

But that won't happen to me.

No way, not my kids.

Maybe one of the reasons Jesus always pointed to children as an example of what it looks like to be a Christian is because a child isn't intimidated by someone who knows everything. Children naturally know how to talk to people who know everything. It's just their reality. This means they're not insecure about looking like they *don't* know everything.

And this, I think, is the humble heart Jesus pointed to when He talked about childlike faith.

It takes a great deal of humility to embrace these two realities in prayer: (1) You don't know everything, and (2) someone else does.

What God is *not* doing is lifting up children as an example because they don't want to know anything. God commands us to love Him with all our "heart, soul, and *mind*" (Matt. 22:37).

The Bible also speaks to the need to move on from the breastmilk that is providing spiritual nourishment for immature believers and begin eating solid food.

> Maybe one of the reasons Jesus always pointed to children as an example of what it looks like to be a Christian is because a child isn't intimidated by someone who knows everything.

The Bible never promotes child*ish* faith; it does promote child*like* faith. I think God upholds children as exemplars because they are humble.

Maybe in the purest sense of the term.

They are fully aware of their needs. They know they can't provide for themselves. They believe and have the capacity by faith to accept all kinds of truth.

This is why even as grown adults, we are still called children of God. Still called to maintain childlikeness. Because we are all helpless.

Take, for example, a mother who prays for her son who is in need of help. God knew before the world was created that this mother would pray for her son and that the son would be in need of help. And God knew all the accompanying circumstances that would bring about the need for prayer.

When God created the world, the circumstances known to Him from before the world began were set in motion. Time itself was set in motion.

The moment arrives when the mother begins to pray for her son, as God knew she would. Even when she was an unformed substance. God meets this mother, comforts her, and listens to her prayer even though He knew every word of the prayer since before the world began.

God's response to her is not to tell her, "I know, I know! I've known about this since before you were an unformed substance!" Instead, He graciously listens and responds. And the mother trusts that God already knows. In fact, there is nowhere else she'd rather go. No one else she'd rather speak to.

Talking to God means she's talking to somebody who knows everything. And so are we.

For God, this doesn't harm or taint the genuineness of the relationship. He is used to this, and, in fact, it is part of God's nature to know everything. Much of embracing the humility needed in prayer is coming to terms with this reality.

In order to justify the need for your prayer, I don't want you to feel as though you have to bring something to God that He is unaware of—as though His unawareness makes the prayer spontaneous and, therefore, more real. When Christians share in their relationship with God, this means that they are communicating with a God who already knows and has been waiting to have this conversation with you ever since you were merely a formless substance.

That shouldn't make prayer seem mundane or unnecessary. It should fill your prayer with anticipation, hope, and awe.

CHAPTER 7

GROANINGS

W hat if I told you groaning was one of the most sacred forms of prayer?

The Greek word *stenagmos* means to groan or sigh. There are only two instances of this word in the New Testament, in Acts 7:34 and Romans 8:26. In both instances, groaning is linked to prayer. And the groaning is humble.

Before we go on, I need to offer my two cents. Thus far, we have looked at some Greek and Hebrew words. As a theology professor, I see a lot of students with biblical words in the original language tattooed on themselves.

My only advice is to make sure you double-check the spelling.

I feel bad being "that guy," letting students know that that is an "interesting" spelling of *faith* or *love* or *abiding* in Greek. Don't trust Google on this one.

Greek tattoos are great. Misspelled Greek tattoos are not.

In Acts 6–7, Luke retells the story with pride of the time when Stephen was doing great wonders and signs among the people. Those listening to Stephen were startled with the wisdom he was speaking by the Spirit.

Clearly unhappy with the attention he was receiving, a bunch of people rose up against Stephen and lied about him, saying that he was contradicting Moses and God. This was a good lie in that it garnered the attention of the religious leaders, who put Stephen on trial. There, Stephen delivered one of the greatest sermons ever recorded.

So convicting, it got him killed.

There is one particular passage in the sermon that I want to look at. It's Acts 7:30–34:

> After forty years had passed, an angel appeared to him in the wilderness of Mount Sinai, in the flame of a burning bush. When Moses saw it, he was amazed at the sight. As he was approaching to look at it, the voice of the Lord came: I am the God of your ancestors—the God of Abraham, of Isaac, and of Jacob. Moses began to tremble and did not dare to look.
>
> "The Lord said to him: Take off the sandals from your feet, because the place where you are standing is holy ground. I have certainly seen the oppression of my people in Egypt; I have heard their groaning and have come down to set them free. And now, come, I will send you to Egypt."

Stephen was pointing back to the time when Moses was in the wilderness of Mount Sinai, and he came upon a bush that was on fire but was not being consumed. As Moses drew near to the bush, the voice of the Lord said, "I am the God of your ancestors—the God of Abraham, of Isaac, and of Jacob" (v. 32a).

Naturally, when Moses encountered a burning bush that wasn't withering away and heard the voice of God coming from that bush, he trembled in fear and turned away. God then responded that it would be appropriate for Moses to remove his sandals as well, because the ground he was standing on was holy. Note: it wasn't the bush that was holy, but the ground. The bush was just helping Moses understand that the ground was holy.

God comforted Moses that He had seen the afflictions caused by the Egyptians and that He had *heard* the Israelites' groanings.

This is important.

The Israelites were experiencing a kind of affliction so great, so overwhelming, that they didn't yet have the words to articulate what they were feeling and experiencing. Yet God's response is that . . . He hears them.

God didn't praise the Israelites for really taking the time to sit down, meditate, and think about how they felt. The Israelites didn't wait until they had the appropriate words to bring before God. No, God heard and understood the language of their groaning, and He came down and saved them.

God helped them because of what He saw and *heard.*

The apostle Paul uses the same word in Romans 8:26. It goes like this: "In the same way the Spirit also helps us in our weakness, because we do not know what to pray for as we should, but the Spirit himself intercedes for us with inexpressible *groanings.*"

Right at the beginning of this verse, Paul highlights that Christians are weak. Weak because they don't know what to pray and, as a result, they don't know which words to employ in prayer.

For Paul, the weakness the Christian suffers from is not a bad thing necessarily—which is interesting because, if Christians were to get stronger, in this context, strength would imply having the knowledge concerning what to pray. That sounds like a good thing. Strength would also indicate that the one praying would have a good handle on the words they might utilize. Again, sounds like a good thing.

Instead, the Christian isn't admonished to go get stronger. Rather, weakness sustains the heart of the Christian in a humble position before the Lord, which then provides the sacred space for the Spirit to help.

Humble people in need seek help. Prideful people think they can do it on their own.

In prayer, prideful people think their words matter. Humble people groan for help.

For Paul, weakness in prayer isn't a problem because humble people recognize their inability, which, coupled with the help from the Spirit, provides the conditions for God to receive prayer. As the Holy Spirit meets the Christian in his or her weakness and intercedes for him or her with groanings too deep for words, God hears and responds.

> Humble people in need seek help. Prideful people think they can do it on their own.

Words are good. They help us communicate all kinds of things. But then humans share a deeper, more intimate form of communication with God. A conversation that goes beyond mere words.

What makes these groanings so deep? Who is the source of these groanings? It's the Holy Spirit.

When something happens in life and you don't have the words to express the sorrow or fear or confusion within, you can be comforted that God still cares.

But how do you know He cares?

Because Paul tells us a Trinitarian prayer is taking place, which doesn't wait for us to figure out what to say. The Holy Spirit intercedes on our behalf in our speechless moment, with groanings too deep for words. These groanings are heard by the Father, through the Son, as a result of the Spirit's help.

In our most vulnerable moments, the triune God is able to carry on a conversation that exceeds human language.

But we don't believe this. At least, we don't live like it.

Instead, we wait until we have the proper words (or so we think) to describe what we are feeling before we go to God in prayer. We believe that God can't hear us until we speak. We believe that God doesn't know until we speak. As a reaction to this fear, we don't pray when we need Him the most.

Yet the moment when we are without words might just be the perfect time to go to God in prayer. It's often in our wordlessness that we are in our most humble, vulnerable, and authentic posture before the Lord.

Am I saying that words don't matter?

Nope.

I just don't want you to wait to pray. I don't want the dust to settle before you pray. I don't want you to feel like God needs your language to be perfectly concise and crystal clear so He can understand you.

God is endlessly resourceful in that He understands all kinds of languages.

Even a wordless language you and I can't make sense of, like groaning.

CHAPTER 8

THOMAS THE
TRAIN UNDIES

Kaden, my older son, lets you know when he is ready to try something new. Lolly is the one who taught me this about him. He has to have the mental space to prepare for something in order for him to be set up for success. You can't just drop some developmental milestone on him and expect him to figure it out.

Lolly is a master teacher with Oliver and Kaden. She knows how they tick.

For Kaden, it typically goes like this. Lolly will tell me that she thinks he is ready to try something new; for example, sleeping in his big-boy bed without a diaper. But she communicates it to Kaden like this:

"Bubba, let me know when you want to try sleeping without a diaper in your big-boy bed."

Then some time later (maybe weeks), the conversation happens.

Kaden: "Momma, I'm ready to try big-boy undies in bed."

Lolly (*without hesitation*): "All right, let's do it."

Me to Lolly: "You sure?"

Lolly to me: "Yes."

Me: "Okay."

Kaden: "I'll go pick out my big-boy underwear."

Kaden then appears in his Thomas the Train undies, ready to take on the challenge.

He goes to sleep that night and, of course, has no accidents. A week goes by, no accidents. Two weeks go by, no accidents. Then one night he comes into our room: "Momma, I'm so sorry! I went potty in my bed. It was an accident. I'm sorry."

His whole countenance said *failure*.

It was like, on the way to our room, he had come to terms with the fact that he will wear diapers for the rest of his life.

Naturally, Lolly and I shamed him and told him to go back to sleep in his bed that he had just gone potty in.

Kidding—*of course* we didn't do that. We scooped him up and told him it was okay, accidents happen, and he will probably do this again at some point! We wanted him to know that we expected him to have an accident in his bed at some point, that accidents are unavoidable when you are learning something new. But he also needed to know that he will have to try again.

Where in the world am I going with this?

When you are learning a new spiritual discipline, there is a great chance it won't come easily to you. Whether you are learning how to fast, tithe, read your Bible, meditate on Scripture—it will feel awkward, unnatural, and uncomfortable.

Prayer is no different.

But why?

I think it's because we underestimate our sin nature and just how much it has affected us. Too often sin nature is taught to Christians as merely affecting our behavior and the actions we perform. This is true, but it's more nuanced and complicated than that.

Sin nature affects us wholly and completely, which, in the case of spiritual disciplines, means that even though we might desire to learn a spiritual discipline, there will be something within us that resists the desire to pray. Honestly, left to ourselves, we might even find ourselves most comfortable not praying.

> We underestimate our sin nature and just how much it has affected us.

That's because your nature, which is corrupt and sinful, has an adverse reaction to spiritual things.

Does that mean you should avoid spiritual things?

No, we just have to be aware that this is what we're up against as we learn, develop, and grow.

You may hear someone else talking about prayer, and they seem like they are talking about an old friend. You might hear them pray and think to yourself that they have no problems at all praying. They know the right words and when to use them. It's like they were created to talk to God. They talk to God all day from the moment they wake up. They probably have volumes of prayer journals full of love letters to God.

Then there is you.

You stutter, fumble, and altogether struggle to put together a group of words that make any sense. You don't know whether to pray to the Father, or the Son, or the Spirit. In fact, you didn't even know you should address them differently (or at all!).

Because of how unnatural prayer is to you, thoughts enter your mind like, *Maybe prayer isn't for me. Maybe it's best if I just let them pray. Maybe prayer isn't my spiritual gift. Maybe there is something really wrong with me.*

No. No. No. No.

When you are learning a new spiritual discipline, you have to factor in failure. You have to factor in how unnatural it will feel at first.

Prayer takes time, and so does learning how to pray. What I mean is that you have to be okay with the discomfort of learning how to pray. In other words, you have to be okay with accidents; you have to be okay with peeing in your Thomas the Train undies.

PART II

PRAYERS OF HUMBLE KINGS

(A STUDY IN 2 CHRONICLES)

*That which brings the praying soul near to God is
humility of heart.
That which gives wings to prayer is lowliness of mind.
That which gives ready access to the throne of grace is
self-deprecation.
Pride, self-esteem, and self-praise effectually shut the
door of prayer.
He who would come to God must approach the Lord
with self hidden from his eyes.
He must not be puffed up with self-conceit, nor can he be
possessed with an overestimate of
his virtues and good works.*
—E. M. BOUNDS

INTRODUCTION
TO PART II

The Old Testament helps lay a foundation for understanding the humility God is looking for in prayer, and our examples of this humility are embodied by two kings.

Have you ever sat down to pray about something important in your life? Or maybe you prayed for someone important in your life and thought to yourself, *I wish God would just tell me what to say, then I would just do that. What to do . . . where to go . . .*

Hidden in the Old Testament is a book called 2 Chronicles. It's within this book that I think God tells you *what* He desires in prayer.

CHAPTER 9

JEHOSHA-WHO?

In 2 Chronicles, we meet a man named Jehoshaphat. The Bible describes him like this:

> Now the LORD was with Jehoshaphat because he walked in the former ways of his ancestor David. He did not seek the Baals but sought the God of his father and walked by his commands, not according to the practices of Israel. So the LORD established the kingdom in his hand. (2 Chron. 17:3–5)

This is significant because about a fourth of the way through 2 Chronicles, toward the end of chapter 9, we find out that Solomon died after reigning for forty years. Other kings reigned after Solomon, but not very many good ones.

Jehoshaphat was a good one.

What made him good was not the things he did, or the armies he led, or the wealth he built; rather, it was his humble heart toward God.

Jehoshaphat was a man known to seek after God and, as a result, the Lord was with him. Here is an example of what I mean.

There was this time when all these -ites were coming to do battle with Jehoshaphat: the Moabites, Ammonites, and Meunites. Their intention was war. Jehoshaphat got word that these men were coming for battle, and since he was the king, I would like to say that his immediate response was to tell those around him not to be afraid, to follow his command and they would be safe. You know, typical king talk.

I would also assume that, since he was such a great king, he had planned for moments just like this. That he had his chosen army, with more supplies than the sand upon the shore. That he had the best and brightest military minds that would be able to strategize from all angles. That his stable of horses was the biggest, healthiest, and strongest in the land. That he had nothing to fear because he was a prepared king.

Actually, it happened a little differently.

Some men came and told Jehoshaphat the news that a large army was preparing for war, and he became very afraid. The Bible says his first response was to seek the Lord. His first command was for the people throughout all Judah to fast.

The people obeyed. They gathered and prayed, and they sought the Lord in all the cities of Judah (2 Chron. 20:1–4).

Then Jehoshaphat didn't retreat to his palace. Rather, he stood in the assembly of Judah, in the house of the Lord, and prayed:

> Lord, God of our ancestors, are you not the God
> who is in heaven, and do you not rule over all
> the kingdoms of the nations? Power and might

are in your hand, and no one can stand against you. Are you not our God who drove out the inhabitants of this land before your people Israel and who gave it forever to the descendants of Abraham your friend? They have lived in the land and have built you a sanctuary in it for your name and have said, "If disaster comes on us—sword or judgment, pestilence or famine—we will stand before this temple and before you, for your name is in this temple. We will cry out to you because of our distress, and you will hear and deliver." (2 Chron. 20:6–9)

King Jehoshaphat understood that he was merely an earthly king, chosen by God to lead heavenly people. He knew all of his own insufficiencies as king, because he personally knew the One who rules all the kingdoms of the nations.

> God, I don't know what to do, but I look to you.

A prideful king would declare, "I've got this; follow me." But King Jehoshaphat prayed, "We do not know what to do, but we look to you" (2 Chron. 20:12).

This is a simple prayer that works in all areas of life. In order to say those words and mean it, you must have a humble heart. Humble people pray, "God, I don't know what to do, but I look to you."

Perhaps, long before we ever get to asking God for something specific, we should be praying like this.

During Jehoshaphat's prayer, all of Judah was standing before the Lord. The Bible says their children were there too. The children were watching their parents seek the Lord. The children were watching their king, who ruled over their mommy and daddy, submit to someone else. Then the Lord responded to the king's prayer: "Do not be afraid or discouraged because of this vast number, for the battle is not yours, but God's" (2 Chron. 20:15).

God was serious—so serious, the Bible says the enemy coming against Jehoshaphat and his people were routed. Annihilated. Crushed. Conquered.

Why did God hear Jehoshaphat's prayer? And what can we learn from his prayer?

These two questions are important, and to answer them appropriately, we have to go back to the beginning. We can't stop in chapter 20. If we do, we'll miss something beautiful about prayer found in 2 Chronicles.

What we will find is that Jehoshaphat's prayer was not random at all. In fact, one might make the argument that 2 Chronicles is a book about prayer. Not just any kind of prayer, though. It's about a humble, God-hearing, God-responding prayer.

So, let's start from the beginning.

CHAPTER 10

THE "CHRONICLER"

Have you ever read 2 Chronicles?

If not, you're in good company. It's often overlooked. It's in the Old Testament, and it's a page-turner with lots of difficult names to pronounce.

When you think about prayer, I bet you don't think about 2 Chronicles, but I hope that changes. This biblical book actually sets the stage for humility, and prayer, and us, and God.

In the book, the "chronicler" (we don't know who wrote 2 Chronicles) is writing on a host of topics, including the Israelites returning from the Babylonian exile, the reign of Solomon, and Judah's fall into sin.

Solomon is a key character. He was King David's son. David was the author of many of the psalms and was called "a man after [God's] own heart" (1 Sam. 13:14). God promised that Jesus would eventually be born through the line of David. Solomon, his son, found favor with God. In fact, many of the promises made to David were fulfilled in Solomon.

Solomon was rich and powerful. He was by far the richest person of his time, and by many accounts he was one of the richest people of all time. Many total his personal fortune to be north of $2 trillion. For just a little perspective, if you were to add up the net worth of the top fifty on *Forbes'* list "The World's Billionaires," that will get you to just over $1.9 trillion. Solomon was richer than the top fifty billionaires in the world today . . . combined.

But I'm interested in reading 2 Chronicles through the lens of prayer, focusing on what God demands from the one praying: humility.

Second Chronicles 7 is really important. It is the climax of the story.

But I have a request: Will you be patient with me?

I think it is necessary for us to start in chapter 1 and walk *slowly* to chapter 7. If we do this the right way, I think you'll appreciate 2 Chronicles more and also learn about God's heart in prayer.

You ready?

The chronicler starts out by establishing Solomon's greatness in his kingdom. We cannot miss that whatever power and influence Solomon had was because God had given it to him. Solomon knew this (2 Chron. 1:1–5).

The chronicler also describes that Solomon went before the Lord at the Tent of Meeting to burn a thousand offerings on the altar (v. 6). That's a lot.

Why is that important?

Because on this same night, God appeared to Solomon, and God asked him to make any request so that He might grant it (v. 7).

So here is our first observation about prayer: if you want to make a request of God and be assured He will give it to you, simply burn a thousand offerings.

Kidding.

That night, Solomon responded to God's offer by first acknowledging the steadfast love He had shown David, Solomon's father. He also recognized that God was the One who made Solomon king over his massive kingdom (vv. 8–9).

But that wasn't it. Solomon did want something. He wanted wisdom and knowledge.

First Kings 4:29–30 describes Solomon this way:

> God gave Solomon wisdom, very great insight, and understanding as vast as the sand on the seashore. Solomon's wisdom was greater than the wisdom of all the people of the East, greater than all the wisdom of Egypt.

Do you think God answered his request?

It's the motivation behind the request that was most important, and the chronicler knew this. He records that Solomon's desire was to lead God's people, and Solomon knew his wisdom and knowledge alone would not be sufficient. He needed more than what he could provide on his own (2 Chron. 1:9–10). Solomon desired heavenly wisdom in order to lead heavenly people.

This book of the Bible is set from the beginning on the foundation of King Solomon's humility before the Lord in prayer. And this humility was not merely a humble behavior.

What do I mean by that?

The Bible says that God responded to Solomon's request and gave him what he asked for. However, God's motivation behind granting the request was also important, and the chronicler knew this too.

It goes like this:

> "Since this was *in your heart*, and you have not requested riches, wealth, or glory, or for the life of those who hate you, and you have not even requested long life, but you have requested for yourself wisdom and knowledge that you may judge my people over whom I have made you king, wisdom and knowledge are given to you. I will *also* give you riches, wealth, and glory, unlike what was given to the kings who were before you, or will be given to those after you." (vv. 11–12, emphasis mine)

It was not merely humble behavior; rather, it was Solomon's humble heart that led God to answer his prayer. And it was Solomon's heart that led God to give him even more than he asked for.

Right at the beginning, God says, "Since this was in your heart."

What was in Solomon's heart? It was humility. He was humble. And because he was humble, so were his prayers.

For some reason, I always thought that Solomon was this king who was the wisest person to ever live. And because he was David's son, he was also very rich due to his inheritance. But the chronicler describes something different—that whatever wealth Solomon had was not because he asked for it. It was not because he was so wise and knowledgeable that he was able to acquire all this wealth. Instead, God gave him riches and wealth, even though he never asked for it (vv. 10–12). God knew that this man was humble enough to handle the wealth He was about to give him.

Then the conversation between Solomon and God ended, and the chronicler simply writes, "and he reigned over Israel" (v. 13).

Next, Solomon, with all his wisdom and wealth, set out to "build a temple for the name of the LORD and a royal palace for himself" (2:1).

The temple would not be modest by any means. (Second Chronicles 3 and 4 are devoted to making this point.) Wouldn't such an ostentatious temple give a bad name to followers of Yahweh? Wouldn't people say, "Why is your church so big and fancy? Why does the temple have to be so ornate? Seems a bit much, don't you think?"

I think part of the reason the temple would be so grand, and beautiful, and awe-inspiring wasn't so that people would turn to Solomon and praise him for the temple he built. Instead, the temple would be God's house, and since God is greater than all the other so-called gods, so was His house (2:5). And whoever was going to build God's house couldn't be concerned about the cost. Money would be no object.

Even as construction was to begin, Solomon was unsure of himself, wondering how he would build a house for God. Please don't miss Solomon's humility—he isn't sure he's capable of accomplishing this great task (v. 6).

In the story, it was another king who encouraged Solomon. His name was Hiram, and he sent Solomon a letter, of all things, encouraging him that he was God's chosen leader to undertake building the temple for the Lord (vv. 11–18).

As a result, the chronicler writes, "Then Solomon began to build the Lord's temple in Jerusalem on Mount Moriah, where the Lord had appeared to his father David" (2 Chron. 3:1). And if you are really interested, construction began in the second month of the fourth year of his reign (v. 2).

By the time we get to 2 Chronicles 5, the temple with all its furnishing is complete. The chronicler writes, "So all the work Solomon did for the Lord's temple was completed" (v. 1).

Are you still with me?

I promise we're going somewhere . . .

CHAPTER 11

IF . . . THEN

Second Chronicles 6 is pretty much one long prayer.

The chronicler sets the stage, describing how after the temple was complete, Solomon stood before the altar of the Lord and, in the presence of all Israel, he prayed a prayer of dedication (v. 12). To properly get a handle on this prayer, let's fast forward to the end of the prayer and then work ourselves back to the beginning. At the very end of the prayer (6:36–40 ESV), Solomon prays,

> "If they sin against you—for there is no one who does not sin—and you are angry with them and give them to an enemy, so that they are carried away captive to a land far or near, yet if they turn their heart in the land to which they have been carried captive, and repent and plead with you in the land of their captivity, saying, 'We have sinned and have acted perversely and wickedly,' if they repent with all their heart

and with all their soul in the land of their cap-
tivity to which they were carried captive, and
pray toward their land, which you gave to their
fathers, the city that you have chosen and the
house that I have built for your name, then hear
from heaven your dwelling place their prayer
and their pleas, and maintain their cause and
forgive your people who have sinned against
you. Now, O my God, let your eyes be open and
your ears attentive to the prayer of this place."

What's going on here?

First, notice that Solomon says, "If they sin against you," as
if there is a possibility that they might not sin against God. But
that isn't what Solomon was going for; instead, it's just the opposite. It is not *if* but *when* you sin against God, which Solomon
goes on to make clear: "for there is no one who does not sin."

In other words, we can't pretend. We all sin. No one is without sin.

Great men and women of prayer are able to make this
humble claim about themselves: they are sinners and they have
messed up.

Furthermore, Solomon described that, as a result of sin, God
became angry and even gave the people over to an enemy so
that they were carried away as a captive to a far land.

This is not good.

So, the proposition before me is not *if* but *when* sin occurs,
God becomes angry and gives me over to my enemy.

You are probably thinking right now, *This is really encouraging, Kyle. There is nothing like being set up for failure.*

Thankfully, the prayer doesn't end there. Not only does the prayer continue, but there are more "ifs" and "thens."

Solomon went on to say: "Yet *if* they turn their heart . . . and repent and plead with you [God] . . . saying, 'We have sinned and have acted perversely and wickedly,' *if* they repent with all their heart and with all their soul . . . and pray . . . *then* hear from heaven your dwelling place their prayer and their pleas, and maintain their cause and forgive your people who have sinned against you" (vv. 37–39 ESV).

Now we need to make some more observations. First, the "yet" of "yet if they turn their heart" is a continuation from the previous verses that transform the bad news into good news.

The bad news is that we all sin, and the result of that sin is God's anger directed toward us. The good news, though, is "yet if" we turn our hearts, pray, and confess our sin, "then" God will forgive us.

> *When* we sin, *if* we turn our hearts, repent, and confess, *then* God will forgive us.

When a phrase starts with "if" in the Bible, typically you will find a "then" lurking around. Often, the "if" is presented to the reader as a choice to make. If you do this, then this will happen. If you don't do this, then this will happen. If you do this, then this won't happen. If you don't to this, then this won't happen.

And for Solomon, the logic goes like this: *when* we sin, *if* we turn our hearts, repent, and confess, *then* God will forgive us.

Solomon's "then" changes everything.

Then God will forgive us.

The "ifs" in Solomon's prayer points to another important observation: some people do not like to be called or think of themselves as sinners. It's offensive. So when they read: "If they sin against you," they conclude that this doesn't apply to them.

Pride prevents us from accepting the reality of our condition as sinners after the Fall. Pride and self-sufficiency trick us into thinking we can obtain an acceptable measure of holiness before God. It goes something like, "But I'm generally a good person. God doesn't think of me as a sinner; after all, I do more good things than bad."

Solomon knew and acknowledged to God that "there is no one who does not sin" (v. 36).

However, some people might still refrain from acknowledging their sin, even to God. That is why Solomon asked God to forgive the people *if* they did, in fact, confess their sin. It also provides the spiritual space for us to live out the lie that we don't sin. Or we could use our words in prayer to confess our sin to God, yet deep down still feel as though what we did wasn't that bad, and maybe we even look forward to committing the same sin again. Of course, in moderation.

That is why Solomon looked beyond the sin, and even beyond the words of prayer, and asked God to hear their hearts, so that if they turned their hearts toward God and confessed their sin, then Solomon asked God to forgive them.

He is really wise, you know?

This takes humility as we confess our sin to God, because we are expressing our inability. It also takes humility to turn our hearts toward the Lord in prayer, because this will likely involve giving up something we desire. Yet in return, we receive forgiveness and a relationship with God.

Remember how we skipped to the end of the prayer? What about the rest of the prayer?

The chronicler first describes a humble King Solomon getting ready to dedicate the temple as he knelt on his knees and spread out his hands toward heaven in full view of all Israel (6:12–13). This powerful king, from his knees, declared that there is no God like Him, in heaven or on earth (v. 14). That God preserved, by His sovereignty, the throne of Solomon's father (David) and was fulfilling the promises made to David through Solomon (vv. 15–16).

Solomon then told God, in view of all the people, that as a mere man, he was insecure at the thought of building a temple that would house God (6:18). Yet Solomon asked God to graciously live in what man had made, and to hear their prayers, and to keep His eyes upon them.

The kind of humble heart that produced these words should not surprise us, because God told us about the kind of heart Solomon had in the very first chapter (2 Chron. 1:11).

Solomon's prayer continues like this:

> *If* a man sins and confesses his sins, *then* hear from heaven and forgive (6:22–23).

> *If* your people sin and confess their sin, *then* hear from heaven and forgive the sin of your people (6:24–25).

> *When* there is a drought in the land caused by sin, and *if* the people pray and confess their sin, *then* hear from heaven and bring forth rain (6:26–27).

> *If* there is a famine, *if* there is pestilence, *if* enemies surround you, *if* plagues, *if* sickness, *then* pray, confess your sin, *then* He will heal (6:28–31).

Solomon prays: "Whatever prayer, whatever plea is made by any man or by all your people Israel, each knowing his own affliction and his own sorrow and stretching out his hands toward this house, *then* hear from heaven your dwelling place and forgive and render to each whose heart you know" (6:29–30 ESV, emphasis mine).

> God will be the judge of your heart.

The only qualifier is that the person praying must be of a humble heart. And God will be the judge of your heart. God alone knows the hearts of the children of mankind.

Solomon's prayer continues.

> *If* an immigrant comes to your land, humbly seeking you [God] with an outstretched arm, *then* hear their prayer and grant their request so that they might make known to all the earth your [God's] great name (6:32–33).

> *If* your people go to battle against their enemies, *then* hear from heaven and give them victory (6:34–35).

Then we get to the end of the prayer, which we talked about at the beginning of this chapter.

> *"If* they *sin against you*—for there is *no one who does not sin*—and *you are angry* with them and give them to an enemy, so that they are carried away captive to a land far or near, yet *if* they *turn their heart* in the land to which they have been carried captive, and *repent* and *plead* with you in the land of their captivity, saying, 'We *have sinned and have acted perversely and wickedly,*' if they *repent* with *all their heart* and with *all their soul* in the land of their captivity to which they were carried captive, *and pray* toward their land, which you gave to their fathers, the city that you have chosen and the house that I have built for your name, *then hear from heaven your dwelling place their prayer and their pleas*, and maintain their cause and *forgive your people* who have sinned against you. Now, O my God, let your eyes be open and your ears attentive to the prayer of this place." (6:36–40 ESV, emphasis mine)

Finally, chapter 7. We made it.

Immediately after Solomon's prayer finished, the chronicler records that fire came down from heaven and consumed the burnt offerings and sacrifices. The glory of the Lord filled the temple, which led the people to bow down and worship, saying, "He is good, for his steadfast love endures forever" (7:3 ESV).

Solomon and the people of Israel dedicated the temple and celebrated for seven days.

Still God did not respond to Solomon's prayer. That is, until the chronicler recorded that during the night the Lord appeared to Solomon.

Side note: for whatever reason, God seemed to respond to Solomon during the night. God did the same thing in chapter 1.

Another side note: it took weeks for God to respond to Solomon's long prayer in chapter 6.

Humble hearts wait weeks for God to respond.

On this night, though, the Lord assured Solomon that He had chosen this temple as His house of sacrifice. God also addressed some of Solomon's prayer, acknowledging not *if*, but *when* due to sin, He shuts up the heavens so that there is no rain, or commands the locusts to devour the land, or sends pestilence among My people, "*If* my people who are called by my name humble themselves, and pray and seek my face and turn from their wicked ways, *then* I will hear from heaven and will forgive their sin and heal their land" (7:14 ESV).

The Hebrew word here for "humble" is *kana*. You can thank me later for your new tattoo idea. In order to understand this Hebrew word, it might be helpful if we reread the sentence and insert some of the other cognates for *kana*. For example:

> "If my people who are called by my name
> bend a knee . . ."

> "If my people who are called by my name
> bring themselves down . . ."

> "If my people who are called by my name
> subdue themselves . . ."

"If my people who are called by my name bring themselves low . . ."

"If my people who are called by my name bring themselves under . . ."

God promises: "*Then* I will hear from heaven . . ."

As long as a person, or a group of people, or a nation, is self-sufficient and arrogant with pride, then God will do nothing for them.

CHAPTER 12

PRETENSE

I remember it so clearly. It was early on with the kids. Lolly came to me and said I was way too hard on Kaden and Oliver.

She said I was getting angry too easily, and I needed to change because it was going to hurt my relationship with them.

Disciplining your children is hard. Knowing when to discipline your children might even be harder. As a parent, I have tried to get better, or as good as I can, at figuring out what kind of heart is driving my boys to do the things they do.

Why? Because it's exhausting constantly correcting behavior. And I'm not sure how loved my kids feel when all I do is say, "No!" Or "Stop!" Or "Go to time-out!"

After all, they are learning for the first time how to use language, walk, use their hands, or run. Things that just months ago they weren't able to do. In that context, it just doesn't make sense to get mad when they yell, or walk in the wrong direction, or don't stop running in the house, or use their dirty hands to draw on the fridge, or make a mess.

Once I trained my mind not to initially look at their actions and instead pay closer attention to their hearts, I began to discipline them differently. To love them differently.

I began to put up with misbehavior and, instead, figure out how to encourage their little spirits, to foster their imagination as they figured out what they could and couldn't do.

In some weird way, I even began celebrating their mistakes. I began to learn that misbehavior, which would have typically earned discipline, was okay, because they weren't always *acting out*; much more often, they were *figuring out* how to behave, how to live.

But they are still children—corrupt and depraved little human beings capable of evil, which means other times their misbehavior warrants discipline.

The trick is figuring out which one it is.

Even in those moments when discipline was called for, I still had to remind myself that they were performing an action that is wrong, but that action was merely a symptom of a larger problem. The misbehavior was just the physical manifestation of something going on inside their little hearts.

Trying to figure out what is going on behind the action is complicated, and the Bible indicates that God is the only One who knows this fully. At times the kids do something wrong from a good heart. Other times, they do sinful things from a bad heart.

Sometimes this is a little easier to adjudicate, like kicking your brother in the face. "Daddy, I didn't do it. My foot did." Sure, kid.

Contemplating the kind of heart that is producing the behavior you see in yourself or others can be applied in all relationships, not just parenting. For example, the church could learn a good lesson here. The church is unfortunately known as a place where you go when you have it all together. Or at least that is how people perceive it.

That means the church is often filled with people who are faking it so that you think they have it all together. As a result, many other people avoid the church because they don't want to feel judged.

What if we loved one another in such a way that, instead of quickly turning to judgment and correction, we turned to the Lord and asked Him to reveal the heart that was producing the action? What if we have been piling on guilt and disciplining followers of Christ who are coming up short but have a good heart? What if they really are trying?

God does discipline. Second Chronicles—and lots of other places in the Bible—makes this clear. But God is also very gracious with those who have a humble heart in the midst of sin. So gracious that discipline is avoided because of someone's humble heart.

For whatever it's worth, it is much easier and more time effective merely to judge the actions you can see being performed. It takes prayer, and time, and some more prayer to figure out what kind of heart is behind the action. (Well, unless they kick someone in the face.)

Let's go back to 2 Chronicles 7:14 (ESV): "If my people who are called by my name humble themselves, and pray and seek my face and turn from their wicked ways, then I will hear from heaven, and forgive their sin, and heal their land."

Did you notice the order in God's response to Solomon?

Remember, this verse isn't talking about a sinless person, but rather one who will commit sin, because "there is no one who does not sin" (2 Chron. 6:36). Yet God graciously says, "Return to Me with a humble heart, and I'll forgive you."

God's overall concern is not the behavior; instead, God looks to the heart. That is not to say God overlooks sin just because the sinner has a humble heart. All sin, even accidental or unknown sin, is punished—but when we humbly repent, it is Christ who bears the punishment, not us. As a result, the sinful action is never above or greater than God's forgiving response. God's grace is always able to match whatever sinful behavior is produced.

It would not have been enough to just say, "Pray, seek My face, and turn from your wicked ways."

Why not?

Those sound like good things to do. Things you might learn in church or a Bible study. Here is the problem: I can do any of those things from an evil, self-sufficient, prideful heart, which according to God in 2 Chronicles, nullifies the good action, no matter how righteous it looks.

Humility—not good actions—is the driving force behind your relationship with God, how you pray, how you seek His face, how you turn from wicked ways.

In other words, the prayer, seeking His face, and turning from wicked ways are actually meaningless—empty, devoid—in and of themselves.

> Humility—not good actions—is the driving force behind your relationship with God.

The Bible has a word for this: *pretense.* It means you fake it really well. You put on a good show.

Hypocrites live a life of pretense. Con artists live a life of pretense.

We find this word in Jeremiah 3:10: "'Yet in spite of all this, her treacherous sister Judah didn't return to me with all her heart—only in pretense [sheqer]'. This is the LORD's declaration."

The Lord, through the prophet Jeremiah, called on Israel and Judah to repent of their sin. The sin Israel and Judah committed is that they played the part of a whore. God brought them into covenant with Himself, like a husband, but they gave themselves to another. They gave their worship to another. They gave their trust to another. They gave their hearts to another. And unless they repented of their sin, God was going to file for divorce.

Jeremiah 3:6 describes it this way: "Have you seen what unfaithful Israel has done? She has ascended every high hill and gone under every green tree to prostitute herself there."

So what happened?

Well, Israel *did not* repent.

Judah, on the other hand, heard Jeremiah's plea and *did* repent—or at least, it looked like they repented. But God wasn't fooled, because Judah only returned to the Lord in *pretense*. Not with all her heart.

God not only rejected this pretense of repentance but actually declared Israel (who didn't repent) to be more righteous than Judah (who did repent). In other words, God preferred no response to a fake one.

If you are anything like me, you've prayed before from a prideful heart, and no one knew it except you. Problem is, I can fool you, but I can't fool God, because He knows my heart.

God knows when I'm praying out of selfish ambitions. God knows when I'm praying in such a way that I'm hoping to manipulate Him into answering my prayer a certain way, to elicit a particular response. God also knows those times when I appear to be seeking His face, but I'm really interested in impressing someone else. Or perhaps I'm seeking His face but more like a salesman trying to get God to buy whatever I'm selling. And sometimes I tell God that I'm turning from my wicked ways, but I know deep down that I'm not ready yet. That I don't intend to change just yet.

God knows these things.

God also knows when my heart is humble in prayer, humbly seeking His face, and humbly turning from wicked ways. God knows this too.

This is why I'm not as concerned with the words we use in prayer, or our posture in prayer, or behavior we might consider employing in prayer. This book isn't about the correct mechanics in prayer, because I don't think they'll get you very far.

If you lack humility, it won't matter.

Prayer that lacks humility is praying in pretense only.

Humility is what God is responding to in our prayerful relationship with Him. As we are humble, He will hear from heaven, forgive sin, and restore our relationship with Him.

> Prayer that lacks humility is praying in pretense only.

You really want to elicit a response from God?

Next time you have something to bring before God in prayer, ask God to reveal your heart. Ask God to help you see the heart behind what you are asking for or about. Once you narrow down the content of your heart, the prayers that spring forth are powerful.

They make things happen.

CHAPTER 13

CONDESCENSION

This study in 2 Chronicles has hopefully led us further toward a belief that prayer happens in its most authentic form when we are humble. Jehoshaphat and Solomon helped us see this in action as they built the foundation of their relationships with God and their involvement within their communities not upon their own privileges as kings, but rather upon the firm foundation of humility.

However, it is important to remember that if we speak at all of humility, we do so as Christians, which means as followers of Christ. As such, we are employing the terms *humble* and *humility* as though they reflect something distinctively Christian. In other words, we are speaking a Christological (the doctrine of Christ) language as we discuss what it means to be humble in prayer.

For Christians, we must look no further than Jesus in order to find our example of humility.

Paul described Christ's humility so beautifully in Philippians 2:5–11 (MSG):

Think of yourselves the way Christ Jesus thought of himself. He had equal status with God but didn't think so much of himself that he had to cling to the advantages of that status no matter what. Not at all. When the time came, he set aside the privileges of deity and took on the status of a slave, became *human*! Having become human, he stayed human. It was an incredibly humbling process. He didn't claim special privileges. Instead, he lived a selfless, obedient life and then died a selfless, obedient death—and the worst kind of death at that—a crucifixion.

Because of that obedience, God lifted him high and honored him far beyond anyone or anything, ever, so that all created beings in heaven and on earth—even those long ago dead and buried—will bow in worship before this Jesus Christ, and call out in praise that he is the Master of all, to the glorious honor of God the Father.

This long passage comes from a letter that the apostle Paul wrote to the church in Philippi. Paul draws the reader's attention to the reality that Jesus Christ is God. The second member of the Trinity. However, Jesus didn't remain in heaven. Instead, He came down to earth in order to save His creation, including humans created in His image.

This is called Christmas.

The Virgin Mary gave birth to a baby—not just any baby, but God Himself. In other words, even though Jesus is equal within the Godhead, Jesus willingly left heaven in order to come down to us. To forgive us. To save us, redeem us, and make a way for us to be adopted by His Father.

Theologically, we have a term for this: *condescension*.

You and I have met condescending people before. They make you feel like you don't belong. Like they are better than you. More important than you. Like when you really need to go to the bathroom and so you walk through the holy threshold from coach to first-class in order to use the lavatory.

Jesus wasn't condescending like that.

Instead, I like the way Glenn Kreider describes condescension in his book, *God with Us*:

> Condescension is intertwined with humility, grace, submission, forgiveness, compassion, looking out for the interests of others, and love. The greatest of all, the transcendent God, cares for his creatures by coming into their world. And he serves them, cares for them, provides for them, obligates himself to them, and loves them.[2]

That's what I mean by condescension.

For God to come down and live among us, He had to leave His position at the right hand of the Father. To describe this act by God, whereby He leaves His position at the right hand of the Father, theologians have another term, *kenosis*, which means "emptied."

Now, you might be thinking, *Wait a second. The second member of the Trinity emptied Himself of His deity to come to earth and die for us?*

---

[2] Glenn R. Kreider, *God with Us: Exploring God's Personal Interaction with His People throughout the Bible* (Phillipsburg, NJ: P&R, 2014), 16.

Not quite.

Jesus, as the second member of the Trinity, did not empty Himself of His deity when He came to earth, but He did empty Himself of His prestige and the privilege of sitting at the right hand of the Father.

In other words, He left heaven as fully God, came to earth retaining His full deity, and was born in our likeness as a human being.

Thus, Jesus Christ was fully human, and fully divine. This *one* person was, and is, 100-percent God and 100-percent man.

Remember that thing about Christian math?

If that isn't humbling enough, Jesus then died the worst kind of death—a crucifixion—so that we might have a relationship with God now and forever.

Within this context of condescension and kenosis, we can understand just a little more what Jesus meant when He said, "No one has greater love than this: to lay down his life for his friends" (John 15:13).

Or Paul admonishing husbands to love their wives "as Christ loved the church and gave himself for her" (Eph. 5:25).

We cannot embody the humility Jesus has modeled for us while remaining prideful. It just doesn't work.

Paul's desire for Christians was that they would "adopt the same attitude as that of Christ Jesus," which was humility (Phil. 2:5).

If humility is the crucial aspect of prayer, Jesus is the model. No one has embodied humility more beautifully, more strikingly, more drastically than He. If we want a more intimate relationship with God in prayer, then we need to take seriously the person of Jesus Christ.

PART III

SIN MAKES YOU HOLY

(A STUDY IN 1 JOHN)

Repentance is not merely the start of the Christian life;
it is the Christian life.

—JOEL BEEKE

INTRODUCTION
TO PART III

To be honest, part III terrifies me. Because if you and I aren't on the same page, then so much will be misunderstood. Thus, this short introduction might be the most important part.

Our topic under discussion is confession. But what do I mean by confession?

Confession is one of our most intimate forms of prayer. For Christians, the term carries a few different meanings.

One way to speak of confession is as it relates to salvation. This means, as humans, we confess that Jesus Christ is Lord, and we believe in Him for the forgiveness of our sins so that we might inherit eternal life.

Paul writes in Romans: "If you confess with your mouth, 'Jesus is Lord,' and believe in your heart that God raised him from the dead, you will be saved" (10:9). This form of confession is inherently linked to one coming to a saving faith in Jesus Christ.

Another way to speak about confession is as it relates to our spiritual life once we *become* Christians. It is this understanding of confession that will be our focus in part III. This kind of confession only relates to salvation in that the one who confesses their sin does so because they are a Christian and want to cleanse themselves of any unrighteousness.

Cleanse themselves of any unrighteousness? Yes, we will get there shortly, but what is so important for now is that you understand there is a difference between confession as it relates to your salvation and confession as it relates to your ongoing relationship with God. Because if you read part III interpreting confession as a means to salvation, you will greatly miss the point.

In part III, the apostle John, also called the disciple whom Jesus loved, will be our teacher and guide back to the light.

CHAPTER 14

THE DISCIPLE HE LOVED

I know you're not supposed to have favorites, but I do, and John is my favorite.

People often say they want to hear a particular sentence spoken over them when they get to heaven. It is a sentence that describes a person at the end of their life right before they enter through the pearly gates.

Do you know what that sentence is?

> Well done . . .
>
> Well done, good . . .
>
> Well done, good and . . .

Many say they want to hear God welcome them with: "Well done, good and faithful servant" (Matt. 25:21a).

There is nothing wrong with that at all, but when I meet Jesus at the end of my life, I'd like to hear something a little different. Something similar to the way the Bible describes John and his relationship with Jesus.

John is often described as "the disciple Jesus loved" (John 21:20). In the Bible, John is not always mentioned by name, yet we know it's John because of the way he's described. For example: "When Jesus saw his mother and *the disciple he loved* standing there" (John 19:26, emphasis mine); and "One of his disciples, *the one Jesus loved,* was reclining close beside Jesus" (John 13:23, emphasis mine). "Peter turned around and saw *the disciple Jesus loved* following them, the one who had leaned back against Jesus at the supper and asked, 'Lord, who is it that's going to betray you?'" (John 21:20).

For some reason, "Well done, good and faithful servant" feels like it has a lot more to do with my behavior, or to put it more Christianly, my works. However, at the end of my life I want to reflect on my relationship with the Lord and not necessarily the things I have accomplished.

Being described as a disciple Jesus loved, just like John, seems to capture a long relationship shared with Jesus, filled with ups and downs, successes and failures.

I think another one of the reasons John is my favorite is that there is something about John that resonates with my heart. It feels like I've known him for a long time. You know that feeling you get when you've never met someone but you just get them? You might even think sometimes, "If we ever met, we'd totally be friends." Lolly and I often think this about Michael Bublé. That's another story, though.

John is a unique figure in the history of Christianity. He was an apostle and one of Jesus' closest friends. He often goes by the epithet "apostle of love," and in many ways his theology was driven by just that: love.

When you read his Gospel, or the three epistles he wrote, or that interesting book called Revelation, one constant on his mind is that we are called to love God and those around us—especially those whom it is difficult to love.

Do you remember a guy named Willard Scott? He was the guy on NBC's *TODAY* show.

In my house growing up, my parents always had the *TODAY* show on in the morning while everyone was eating breakfast and getting ready to go to work or school. For some reason, I always paid attention to Willard's segment on the show.

He would come on the television and wish people who had just turned one hundred years old (or older!) a happy birthday. A picture of these people would always appear on the television, and Willard would read their advice for living a long life.

Often it was something short and sweet, like, "Don't go to bed angry," "Stay active," "Always kiss your wife good night," "Read your Bible and pray every day," or "Eat lots of junk food."

There is something beautiful about the simplicity of aging wisdom. Not because the one aging isn't wise enough for the complex thoughts of life. Rather, they have lived so long, thought so hard, that at the end of life they are able to take complex wisdom and simplify it to just a few words in a profound way.

The apostle John was similar. While he did live close to one hundred, he didn't quite make it—which means he was never on the *TODAY* show with Willard Scott. But church history does attribute this one saying to John that often runs through my mind; it's something he said later in life: "My little children, love one another." And when asked why, he would say, "It is the Lord's command, and if this alone be done, it is enough."

So this man was an apostle. One of Jesus' closest friends. Who saw the resurrected Lord. Witnessed the transfiguration. Saw all the miracles performed by Jesus.

You're telling me his final message to people near the end of his life was, "Love one another"?

As this study in 1 John begins, this is the phrase I want fresh in our minds.

By the way, John didn't make up the phrase "love one another." He listened well to the words of Jesus, because Jesus was obsessed with loving God and others.

Matthew records a moment when Jesus was interacting with the Pharisees and Sadducees. In fact, it was rather contentious. The Bible describes the Pharisees and Sadducees as plotting to trick Jesus so that they could bring a charge against Him. The trick came in the form of a question: "Teacher, which command in the law is the greatest?" (Matt. 22:36)

This is a loaded question, because there is a lot in the law. Like, 613 various dos and don'ts. How was Jesus going to possibly answer this question without leaving out an important law from Moses or the prophets?

But here is Jesus' response: "Love the Lord your God with all your heart, with all your soul, and with all your mind. This is the greatest and most important command" (vv. 37–38). And Jesus didn't stop there. He added: "The second is like it: Love your neighbor as yourself. All the Law and the Prophets depend on these two commands" (vv. 39–40).

There it is: the greatest commandment in all the law is to love God and your neighbor.

But I thought the Pharisees and Sadducees asked Jesus for just one commandment—the greatest *commandment* in all the law? Why did Jesus give two?

Let's not miss that Jesus' command was singular. It was love. That's the command. Jesus just directs that love in two different directions.

This is beautiful, but there is still another observation that needs to be made. It has to do with diapers.

Well, not really.

In verse 40 Jesus says, "All the Law and the Prophets *depend* on these two commands." The word *depend* is interesting. In the Greek, depend (*krematai*) has very little to do with a brand of adult diapers. Another way you could translate "depend" here is to say, "All the Law and the Prophets *hang* on these two commands." Just like a heavy door hangs on its hinges, so do the law and prophets hang on these two commandments.

For Jesus and His friend John, instead of obsessing over all the law and prophets, if one were to simply love God and those around them, it would, in a profound way, fulfill the law and prophets.

So John clearly got this theology of love from Jesus. But Jesus didn't make up this commandment either. Actually, what makes His answer to the Pharisees and Sadducees so beautiful is that He didn't change anything; instead, He merely echoed the Old Testament, with which they would have been very familiar.

Jesus restated in the form of a commandment a confession called the Shema from the Old Testament, which goes like this:

> "Listen, Israel: The LORD our God, the LORD
> is one. Love the LORD your God with all your
> heart, with all your soul, and with all your

strength. These words that I am giving you today are to be in your heart. Repeat them to your children. Talk about them when you sit in your house and when you walk along the road, when you lie down and when you get up. Bind them as a sign on your hand and let them be a symbol on your forehead. Write them on the doorposts of your house and on your city gates." (Deut. 6:4–9)

This confession of faith was recited daily—twice a day, actually—in the morning and evening. In many ways, reciting this confession grounded the confessor and helped to simplify the objective for the day. Then, at the end of the day, it provided sacred space for the confessor to contemplate and thank the Lord for the many blessings of the day.

In other words, it gave the confessor the chance to ask whether God was loved above all.

Thus, Jesus' answer to the Pharisees and Sadducees was not new or novel. He simply reminded them of an important confession they had learned from their youth. To love.

There is a Christian expression that has been used (maybe even misused) so much that it doesn't mean a whole lot anymore. It goes like this: As Christians we aren't about a religion, we are about a _____.

Yep, *relationship.*

In fact, it's our emphasis on relationship that is supposed to set Christianity apart from all the other religions. However, I'm not so sure it has set us apart for the right reasons. What I mean is that Christians have not modeled relationship well with one another, so it doesn't ring as true when we confess it to the world around us.

It would be like me emphasizing how important my marriage is—all the while constantly treating my wife poorly. Wouldn't you doubt how important my marriage really is to me?

I want to recapture this relationship with God that we say we're all about. I'm not interested in, nor do I really even care about, confession of sin that is for ceremonial purposes only. For religious purposes only. Anyone can do that.

Confession isn't merely an action, whereby we just do the right thing.

I think that is why the Pharisees and Sadducess asked the question they did. They wanted to know what was the most important thing they should *do* as leaders in their religion. They only cared about the action.

They probably debated this question all the time among themselves.

Yet Jesus didn't care. He wanted them to confess their love to God from a genuine, humble heart, and then to love those around them. And when this was done, they didn't need to worry about the other stuff as much. It would fall in line.

John, like Jesus, desired that his disciples love the Lord and live in relationship with Him.

As we are about to see, this is accomplished through confession.

CHAPTER 15

COMPLETE JOY

John begins his short letter (1 John) talking about joy. Not a kind of joy that just anyone can have, but a distinctly Christian joy. This is an exclusive kind of joy, that anyone who believes in the Lord experiences.

What makes Christian joy so unique? Well, according to John it's a complete kind of joy.

Complete?

Yes, complete.

He says, "We are writing these things so that our joy may be complete" (1 John 1:4). We are going to get to "these things" in a moment, but first we have to ask, what does "complete" even mean?

Technically, *complete* here means to render something completely full. It's like a glass filled to the brim, without room to add even a drop of water.

For John, to have a full-to-the-brim relationship means that it's a complete relationship. For example, in another letter he talks about his physical connection with the reader. John says,

"Though I have many things to write to you, I don't want to use paper and ink. Instead, I hope to come to you and talk face to face so that our joy may be complete" (2 John 12).

In other words, ink and paper is far from a full relationship. For John, living life with them, in their presence, face-to-face, would be the most fulfilling.

This is no different with God. A person is most joyful when in a close relationship with God (1 John 1:3–4). Not because of how "Christianly" they act or speak, but because they are in a healthy spiritual relationship with God.

But does that mean it's possible to have a bad relationship with God? Yes. In fact, that is exactly where John is taking us.

He is building an argument, and the foundation of his argument is inherently relational. Which for John, must include prayer. Confessionary prayer, to be exact.

However, he doesn't want to confuse the act of confession with merely doing something. No. Because remember, the foundation of his argument is relational, not meritorious.

John's greatest desire is for Christians to love God and have good relationships with God—healthy, complete, joyful relationships.

Notice John's preamble to this letter. In the first few verses we read that it's the close relationship he has with Jesus that is the basis for his authority and why the audience should believe what he's about to say. It's like he's pleading with the reader: *Listen to us!* As apostles we've heard Jesus (v. 1), seen Him with our own eyes (vv. 1–2), touched Him with our own hands (vv. 1–3), and we want to tell you everything we know (v. 3).

And for the present purpose, John wants to tell the reader everything he knows about having a relationship with God.

Notice how John doesn't appeal to his own life as to why the reader should listen to him and the other apostles. Instead, it is based on Jesus and their relationship with Him.

But what does this relationship with God look like?

For the disciple whom Jesus loved, a relationship with God is like walking in the light.

He writes,

> This is the message we have heard from [Jesus] and declare to you: God is light, and there is absolutely no darkness in him. If we say, "We have fellowship with him," and yet we walk in darkness, we are lying and are not practicing the truth. If we walk in the light as he himself is in the light, we have fellowship with one another, and the blood of Jesus his Son cleanses us from all sin. (vv. 5–7)

Why the light?

Because "God is light and in him is no darkness at all" (v. 5 ESV). Somewhere else in the Bible another writer describes God's light like this: "Every good and perfect gift is from above, coming down from the Father of lights, who does not change like shifting shadows" (James 1:17).

This means that if we really want to have a relationship with God, we must meet God on His terms—in the light.

In other words, meeting God on His terms only works if we are humble enough to recognize who we are in light of who God is.

There is no darkness in God, which means when we are walking in darkness we are relationally at a distance from God. He hasn't abandoned us, but we've distanced ourselves.

What, then, does it look like for a Christian to walk in darkness?

Later in his letter John writes: "But the one who hates his brother or sister is in the darkness, walks in the darkness, and doesn't know where he's going, because the darkness has blinded his eyes" (1 John 2:11).

In other words, walking in the darkness is related to the condition of one's heart and the ways in which Christians don't live up to Jesus' theology of love.

> Meeting God on His terms only works if we are humble enough to recognize who we are in light of who God is.

Remember the greatest commandment? To love God with all your heart, soul, and mind. And also, to love your neighbor as yourself. It's a lack of love that reveals your darkness. For John, when someone hates another Christian, this reveals a long walk in darkness.

I want to return to a few verses and then make some more observations. Remember when John said: "If we say, 'We have fellowship with him,' and yet we walk in darkness, we are lying and are not practicing the truth. If we walk in the light as he himself is in the light, we have fellowship with one another, and the blood of Jesus his Son cleanses us from all sin" (1 John 1:6–7).

A humble heart admits when it has *walked* in darkness.

A humble heart admits when it is *walking* in darkness.

A prideful heart sees a challenge, and the challenge is to always walk in the light. The prideful heart is self-righteous and confident that it needs no help avoiding the darkness.

Here's the humble reality: walking in the light with any measure of consistency is not a reality that many (if any!) can achieve.

So what do you do?

The challenge, then, is no longer to walk in the light; the game now is how well can you fake it.

The challenge becomes: How good at looking like light are you?

To borrow the language from an earlier chapter, we portray the pretense of light to make others think we're walking in the light when, in reality, we're not.

Once we begin to accept this difficult reality, things like social media begin to make more sense.

It seems like every few months, Lolly and I discuss giving up on social media—just canceling our accounts and going back to life prior to posts, updates, news, and photos.

You've seen this, right? That person on social media who is "taking a break," or, to put it more spiritually, "fasting" from social media.

To be fair, though, there are a lot of beautiful interactions on social media too, which is why we never end up deleting our accounts. I can't tell you how many former students I'm able to stay in touch with, pray with, or discuss further education and ministry with via social media. Lolly and I love keeping up with our friends who live far away and seeing their kids grow up right before our eyes.

However, in those moments when we want to give up on social media, our conversation seems always to get back to the dissatisfaction with the honesty (or lack thereof) with which people portray their lives. As though they have the perfect kids, marriage, church, job, everything!

The attraction is so strong that we can get wrapped up in it too. And yet, we know it's not real. We know this because we are friends with these people. We know this because we know our own lives. Yet there is a sense in which social media tempts us to put forth the pretense that life is all light and in it is no darkness at all.

If that is the case, should it surprise us when people are just as good at portraying their relationships with God as always being in the light?

Before we keep going, you have a humbling decision to make.

A humbling decision? Yes.

According to John, God is light, and if you desire to have a relationship with God, you must walk in the light.

How is walking in the light possible? You have three options:

> **Option 1:** Walking in the light is possible through a Christian's continual obedience to the Lord, which means you have no darkness to worry about. Good luck. I'll be praying for you.

> **Option 2:** You can fake it and keep up the exhausting effort of living a life with the pretense of light. Only to fool yourself and those around you, but never God.

Option 3: You can try your best to love God and those around you, but you can also be humble and confess those moments when you are walking in the darkness.

If you're content with options 1 and 2, John is not going to make much sense at all to you. If anything, John is going to try to convince you that option 1 is theologically untenable. I also think he wants to free you from your life of holy pretense, which comes to light as you find complete joy in your gracious relationship with God.

If you like option 3 but don't quite know what it means to "be humble and confess," that's okay. In fact, at this point, that's a good place to be.

Right now, you might even begin to feel some cracks in your foundation, which were constructed on the facade of having it all together, especially as it relates to your relationship with God.

Don't worry, though—that's by design. I want some of your foundation to crack. And remember, I told you I wasn't going to leave you throughout this adventure.

It's also possible that you've been so confused lately, questioning the genuineness of your relationship with God, maybe even doubting whether God exists, because you feel like you are doing all the right things and yet you've never felt so far away from God. Hang in there, because the next few chapters might prove to be sacred ground.

CHAPTER 16

FORGET PERFECT

Have you ever noticed that it is totally acceptable to talk about how sinful you were before you were a Christian? It's almost like the more sinful you were, the better the story.

Christians call this type of story a testimony, which is simply a retelling of how someone came to believe in Jesus Christ as their Lord and Savior.

What's sad is that some Christians are insecure, even discouraged, because they don't have as "good" of a testimony as someone else. It's like they feel as though they don't have as meaningful of a relationship with God as the person who dramatically came to believe in the Lord.

Socially, it's common when Christians meet one another to share the story of how they became a Christian. These are supernatural stories that we tell. They're unique, personal, and truly necessary. They're cause for giving thanks.

This is why I get sad, maybe even a little defensive, when before a Christian shares his or her testimony, he or she prefaces it with: "Well, my testimony isn't like *her* testimony, but . . ."

Translation: my story isn't as good as hers.

Have you ever heard this before? Maybe even said this yourself?

Each story of how a person came to know the Lord is beautiful and unique. Just like your fingerprint. Or your sneeze. Your testimony is uniquely yours, and it should be told often.

If Christians are generally quite open about sharing their past sin, why does it seem like that all changes when we become Christians? All of a sudden, it's now taboo to talk about your sinfulness and mistakes. You can talk about your past failures, but don't you *dare* bring up present struggles.

Why is this?

Seriously, someone answer this for me.

The disciple Jesus loved tried to change this Christian cultural perception.

I use the language "Christian cultural perception" on purpose, because the world around us is still fully aware of the continued sinfulness of Christians, even after their conversion. It's only Christians who pretend like we don't sin anymore.

> I think some people have stayed away from Christianity because they find it odd that Christians pretend they aren't sinners anymore.

In fact, I think some people have stayed away from Christianity because they find it odd that Christians pretend they aren't sinners anymore. If Christians are hiding that, what else might they be hiding?

Okay, let me ask: Have you ever messed up? There is no way around it, and you just need to admit it.

And have you ever said something like this in response? "Look, I'm not a perfect person." "I'm not perfect, but neither are you." "I understand that I'm not perfect." "Sorry, I'm human, not perfect."

I've said this before. A bunch of times.

Then it hit me: "Kyle, you're not perfect? Of course, you aren't perfect. You're not even *good!*"

Think about it. What are we trying to communicate when we use this expression to explain why the person shouldn't be so mad at us? Whether we are aware of it, what is communicated is that you are a really, really good person, but unfortunately, you're just shy of perfection.

And since you're a really, really good person, just not a perfect person, they shouldn't be so hard on you.

Here's the thing: this is true; you and I aren't perfect. But is that going far enough? What if you and I are not just far from perfect, but we're far from good?

You might be thinking, *Wait a second. You want me to say I'm not a good person? That's kind of offensive. But I help people all the time. I open doors for people. If I see trash on the ground, I typically pick it up. If someone sneezes, I always say, "Bless you." Wait, no, I say, "God bless you." I go to church every Sunday. I serve in the youth group. I host a small group.*

I'm convinced that when you pray from a humble posture before God, from a humble heart, those prayers change the world around you. But in order to pray from that humble posture, you need to admit that you aren't holy. That you aren't perfect. Nor are you good.

You can't fake humility, because God knows your heart perfectly. Even though you might be able to trick someone else around you and conceal your pride as though you're humble, you can't mislead God.

The condition of humankind after the Fall—remember, Adam and Eve were naked and ashamed—wasn't that they lacked perfection; rather, they lacked goodness.

The apostle Paul describes our lack of goodness in a letter he wrote called Romans. He even quotes a bunch of Old Testament verses to support his theology concerning humankind. Hold on, though, because it's rather harsh. He writes:

> What then? Are we any better off? Not at all! For we have already charged that both Jews and Greeks are all under sin, as it is written:
>
> > There is no one righteous, not even one.
> > There is no one who understands;
> > there is no one who seeks God.
> > All have turned away;
> > all alike have become worthless.
> > There is no one who does what is good,
> > not even one.
> > Their throat is an open grave;
> > they deceive with their tongues.
> > Vipers' venom is under their lips.
> > Their mouth is full of cursing and bitterness.
> > Their feet are swift to shed blood;
> > ruin and wretchedness are in their paths,
> > and the path of peace they have not known.
> > There is no fear of God before their eyes.
> > (Rom. 3:9–18)

We use these kinds of excuses: "Look, I'm not a perfect person." "I'm not perfect, but neither are you." "I understand that I'm not perfect." But maybe it would be more accurate if we said, "Look, I'm not a good person." "I'm not good, but neither are you." "I understand that I'm not good."

Does it really demand that much humility to admit you aren't perfect? I don't think so. But confessing that you aren't good? That is a humbling thing to admit.

What I'm not saying is that you never do anything good. Christians do good things all the time. Even people who don't profess a faith in Jesus Christ do good things. However, saying that someone does good is one thing; saying someone is good is a whole different claim.

In 1 John, the disciple Jesus loved is talking about a relationship with God. But remember, not in a salvation sense here; rather, he was thinking about after someone becomes a Christian. And specifically, John is talking about maintaining a relationship with God, who demands that we walk in the light.

John would rather you be realistic and not believe the lie that you are a good person, or in other words, that you consistently walk in the light. Rather, I think he would prefer you to be humble enough to admit you aren't good. That you sin. You mess up. Way more than you do good.

And when you sin, you walk in the darkness, which means your relationship with God isn't good.

That sounds a bit depressing, right? But it's not. Because once you believe this and understand this, John has good news. But unless you believe in your lack of goodness, you won't understand the good news.

Throughout the next few chapters, we are going to discuss the idea of confession, and when we do, 1 John 1:9 is going to help us a lot.

It's a verse that is full of good news to the Christian who is humble enough to admit they aren't good. The verse says: "If we confess our sins, he is faithful and righteous to forgive us our sins and to cleanse us from all unrighteousness."

But the disciple Jesus loved does something really interesting with verse 9. He surrounds the good news (1 John 1:9) with two verses that demand humility (1 John 1:8, 10).

Or to say it another way, John surrounds the good news with two verses that would likely scare off a prideful heart because they contain such bad news.

First John 1:8–10 goes like this: "If we say, 'We have no sin,' we are deceiving ourselves, and the truth is not in us. If we confess our sins, he is faithful and righteous to forgive us our sins and to cleanse us from all unrighteousness. If we say, 'We have not sinned,' we make him a liar, and his word is not in us."

In biblical studies, there is a term that describes what John is doing. It's called an *inclusio*.

In addition to being a fun word to say, an inclusio is a literary framing device where you employ the same word or phrase or idea at the beginning and end of a section.

Often, what the writer is doing is drawing your attention to what is in the middle of the incluiso.

Since in the Greek language of this period (the language John wrote in) there weren't verses and paragraphs, John had to be creative with how he was going to get the reader to pay attention to what was important. In 1 John 1:8–10, John forms an inclusio with the phrase, "If we say, 'We have no sin'" from verse 8 and "If we say, 'We have not sinned'" from verse 10. Look back up at those verses, and you'll see it.

If you really want to understand the good news and what John means when he says, "If we confess our sins, he is faithful and righteous to forgive us our sins and to cleanse us from all unrighteousness" (v. 9), you first need to confess you are a sinner (vv. 8, 10).

Not a past sinner with a great testimony, but a sinner who still walks in darkness. Not because you want to walk in the darkness, but because as a sinner it's really hard not to walk in darkness.

Christians able to make this kind of confession concerning themselves are well on their way to holiness.

CHAPTER 17

YOU LOSER

My personal philosophy is you haven't achieved the essence of being a parent until your child calls you a loser.

This was a parental milestone for me. You know, a real high point.

It was a few years ago now; Oliver wasn't born yet. I was at home for lunch with Lolly and Kaden. It was very common in the afternoon for Kaden to play while Lolly got his lunch ready.

I remember talking to Lolly while Kaden was playing with a basketball. He threw the ball in my direction and, apparently, I wasn't paying close enough attention to him, because out of nowhere Kaden said, "You loser!"

Lolly and I looked at each other as if to say, "What the heck did he just say?" Then I asked Lolly, "Did he just call me a loser?"

I immediately told him to go to time-out. Lolly started the timer, which was two minutes. It was as though we had two minutes to figure all of parenting out.

Looking back, it was a funny two minutes as Lolly and I scrambled to figure out what our next steps as parents were going to be.

Do we take away something he loves? Do we search for boarding schools?

Where did he learn this anyway? Were we unknowingly walking around calling people losers all the time? It was so out of character for Kaden to talk like that.

The timer went off. Lolly walked over to Kaden, knelt down to his level, and asked him why he was in time-out. Kaden told Lolly in a whisper that he called Daddy a loser. Lolly told Kaden to go over to Daddy and say he was sorry.

Then Kaden came over to me, head down, feeling awful, and he just said, "Sorry, Daddy."

I knelt down and asked what he was sorry about. I really wanted him to confess to me what he'd done. Not just give me a generic "sorry." He couldn't tell me, though. He didn't remember, he said. But really, he didn't want to tell me. It was almost like he didn't want to say it out loud again.

He ran back over to his mom and started crying. Lolly calmed him down and asked why he was crying, and he told her he was too afraid to tell me. Kaden said he was too afraid that I wouldn't forgive him.

There are probably lots of reasons why someone might not want to confess their sin to God. But if I had to guess, Kaden captures some of our fears—that we are too scared that God won't forgive us if we actually tell Him what we've done.

As though He doesn't know what we've done until we tell Him.

As a result, we hide (or so we think) from God. We pretend like it didn't happen. We make a personal commitment, a deal with ourselves, not to do that again.

And if you just avoid it long enough, it seems like the guilt goes away.

Or maybe you think that, because you are a Christian, that means Jesus has already died for your sins, so you don't need to confess your sin anymore.

However, John learned from Jesus that in order to have a relationship with Him you need to walk in the light. This is difficult because we aren't prefect. Actually, we aren't even good.

John is gracious in his teaching. He doesn't want Christians to try to hide the reality that we are sinners. Instead, he says things like, "If we say, 'We have no sin,' we are deceiving ourselves, and the truth is not in us" (1 John 1:8).

And he says, "If we say, 'We have not sinned,' we make him a liar, and his word is not in us" (v. 10).

John actually provides the sacred space for Christians to honestly be themselves, even if that means at times (many times!) we sin and walk in the darkness. It is quite a vulnerable feeling to stand before someone, completely exposed.

This is beautiful and a great example for Christians as we seek to love one another. One of the distinctive qualities of a Christian should be our love for people just as they are. Even when they are walking in the darkness.

Why still love them?

Because God loves you when you walk in darkness.

John provides this sacred space because he knows there is a remedy to darkness. It would be a completely different story if he didn't have a cure. But he knows how to return to the light and once again enjoy a close relationship with God.

He writes: "If we confess our sins, he is faithful and righteous to forgive us our sins and to cleanse us from all unrighteousness" (v. 9). This means that when a Christian prays, and confesses their sin, God promises to be faithful and to forgive them.

According to John, there is no need for a Christian to wonder *if* God will forgive them.

No reason to be fearful that God *might not* accept them. Instead, there is freedom knowing that God *will* forgive the one who confesses their sin.

John goes on to say that, in addition to forgiveness, the Christian is cleansed from all unrighteousness.

Cleansing here references ritual cleansing, but not the cleansing that would have taken place in the Old Testament.

> There is no need for a Christian to wonder *if* God will forgive them. No reason to be fearful that God *might not* accept them.

Instead, John looks to Jesus to cleanse the Christian who confesses their sin.

He writes: "If we walk in the light as he himself is in the light, we have fellowship with one another, *and the blood of Jesus his Son cleanses us from all sin*" (v. 7, emphasis mine).

God offers forgiveness and cleansing to Christians walking in the dark. All that is required is the humility to know in your heart that you have sinned and the humility to confess that sin to God.

As a result, one is able to walk in the light again.

And again.

And again.

And . . .

This verse contains some uncertainty, though—but not as it relates to God. Rather, the uncertainty is directed toward the one walking in darkness.

The only way the unrighteousness remains is when it is left unconfessed.

Did you notice the very first word in 1 John 1:9? John says: "*If* we confess our sins . . ."

If.

That means there is the possibility that we might not confess our sin.

In other words, that we continue to walk in the darkness. Or, to say it another way, all the unrighteousness remains when we refuse to confess our sin.

It takes humility to confess your sins to God, and yet when you go to God in confession, He never returns your humility with humiliation. God will never hear your confession and shame you in return. More on this later.

Sadly, too many Christians are more than willing to avoid a spiritual confrontation with God in confession and instead opt to let unrighteousness remain. To let darkness set in.

What's strange about darkness is that you can actually walk in it—but only if you let your eyes adjust to the darkness first.

One of my favorite things to do is lie down with the boys at night before they fall asleep. We whisper and talk until Mommy yells from the other room, "Daddy, they need to go to sleep!" For some reason, I must hear "Go to sleep!" because I always seem to wake up at midnight and make my way to our room.

It never fails, though: when I wake up, I can see everything in their room. I can see the door, my phone, their toys, everything.

This works spiritually too. The more time you spend in the dark, the better you can see over time.

The Gospel of Mark includes a beautiful story about confession, and it involves the disciple Jesus loved. Notice the pride and humility in the story. Notice the conversation between John and Jesus.

In the beginning of Mark 9 Jesus told the disciples that some of those standing with Him would not die before they see the power of the kingdom of God (v. 1).

The Gospel then describes that six days later Jesus took James, Peter, and John with Him to a high mountain. It was there on the mountain that something supernatural happened: Jesus was transfigured before them (v. 2). Before these three disciples, the Son of God took on the form of His heavenly glory.

The Bible describes it like this: "his clothes became dazzling—extremely white as no launderer on earth could whiten them" (v. 3).

Elijah and Moses appeared to them and started talking to Jesus (vv. 4–5).

Then a voice came out of the cloud:, "This is my beloved Son; listen to him!" (v. 7).

And then suddenly, everyone was gone; James, Peter, and John saw no one standing with Jesus. His clothes were back to normal as if nothing happened (v. 8), and yet they were probably thinking to themselves, *What in the world was that?*

On the way back down the mountain, Jesus told them not to say anything until after the Son of Man rose from the dead (v. 9).

The disciples agreed and then spent the rest of the walk try-ing to figure out what this "rising from the dead" thing meant (v. 10).

As the disciples and Jesus neared the bottom of the moun-tain, they came to the other disciples and saw a great crowd around them. The Bible says the disciples were arguing with the scribes, who were among the religious leaders of the day (v. 14).

That's all the Bible says about that. They were arguing.

Then the entire crowd saw that Jesus was nearby, and they ran up to greet Him.

When the crowd got close enough, Jesus asked them: "What are you arguing with them about?" (v. 16).

A father from the crowd spoke up and answered Jesus. We come to find out that the disciples weren't arguing with the scribes about a particular question; they were arguing about a scenario, which was playing out right before them.

The father said to Jesus: "Teacher, I brought my son to you. He has a spirit that makes him unable to speak. Whenever it seizes him, it throws him down, and he foams at the mouth, grinds his teeth, and becomes rigid. I asked your disciples to drive it out, but they couldn't" (vv. 17–18).

The Bible then says that Jesus answered "them," which means He didn't just answer the father, but the whole crowd, including the disciples, scribes, the father, the boy, and the demon. "You unbelieving generation, how long will I be with you? How long must I put up with you? Bring him to me" (v. 19).

The Bible describes a scene in which the boy was brought before Jesus, and immediately when the evil spirit saw Jesus, it caused the boy to convulse, fall on the ground, and roll around, foaming at the mouth (Mark 9:20).

Jesus asked the father how long this had been going on, and the father replied, "From childhood" (v. 21). The father then asked Jesus for help. In a real way, he prayed for help: "If you can do anything, have compassion on us and help us" (v. 22).

Jesus' response to the father was: "'If you can'? Everything is possible for the one who believes" (v. 23).

Then Jesus rebuked the unclean spirit and said to it, "You mute and deaf spirit, I command you: Come out of him and never enter him again" (v. 25).

The demon left and didn't come back.

Then, like so many other times in the Gospels, the disciples got Jesus alone and asked Him privately what they would be too embarrassed to ask publicly: Why couldn't they cast the demon out of the child? Jesus' response to them was: "This kind can come out by nothing *but prayer*" (v. 29).

The father got this right. He humbly *prayed* to God. The disciples didn't. They pridefully thought they had the ability to remove this demon on their own. After all, they were Jesus' disciples.

Remember when Jesus rebuked them and said, "You unbelieving generation, how long am I to be with you? How long must I put up with you?" (v. 19). It wasn't necessary for Jesus to be present in order to drive this demon out of the child. The disciples could have driven it out, but not with their own power; not merely with their own words. They needed to invoke the name of Jesus through prayer. They needed to pray and ask God to remove this demon on their behalf.

However, their pride was stronger than their desire to see this little boy healed. They didn't have the humility to ask for help. They wanted the crowd to see how great they were, the scribes to know who could do the miraculous. And Jesus reminded them that this kind of demon can only be driven out by prayer.

In other words, this kind of demon could only be driven out by humility.

Later, Mark tells us the disciples were staying with Jesus in a house in Capernaum. There at the house Jesus asked them: "What were you discussing on the way?"

Jesus often did this in the Gospels: He asked questions He already knew the answer to.

The disciples didn't say a word, because on the way to the house they were arguing with one another about who was the greatest.

They wouldn't tell Jesus what they were talking about, but He already knew—and He responded to their argument with the help of a little child.

Jesus said: "If anyone wants to be first, he must be last and servant of all" (v. 35).

Then the Bible describes Jesus putting His arms around a little child and saying, "Whoever welcomes one little child such as this in my name welcomes me. And whoever welcomes me does not welcome me, but him who sent me" (v. 37).

The disciples had it all wrong. They wanted to know who was the greatest, and Jesus wanted to know who was willing to heal the little child from earlier in the day.

I think that is what Jesus meant when he said, "Whoever welcomes one little child such as this in my name welcomes me. And whoever welcomes me does not welcome me, but him who sent me" (v. 37).

In other words, the disciples tried to save this child with their own great names, and yet their own great names could not heal this child. They should have prayed in the name of Jesus for this child to be healed, because when one receives Jesus, one also receives Jesus' Father.

Then John, the disciple Jesus loved, said something to Jesus. John did not ask a question. John did not answer a question. John offered a confession to Jesus: "Teacher, we saw someone driving out demons in your name, and we tried to stop him because he wasn't following us" (v. 38).

John got it. He realized the sin they committed, and he confessed it to Jesus.

Remember earlier when they came down the mountain to find everyone arguing (v. 14)?

We are never let in on what the disciples and scribes were arguing about, but I have a guess. I think the scribes were trying to cast out the demon by calling upon the name of Jesus, and the disciples were rebuking them for it. The disciples were probably telling the scribes that they can't call upon the name of Jesus. Why? Because the scribes weren't followers of Jesus like them.

This was the power play the disciples were making over the scribes in order to demonstrate their greatness. That *only* they could cast out demons—not the scribes, not the crowd. Only the disciples.

And what was so embarrassing is that they couldn't—which only fueled their pride and desire to figure out who was the greatest.

They probably thought to themselves: *If we can just figure out who is the greatest, then the next time we encounter a demon like this, we'll have that disciple cast it out.*

John humbly confessed his sin—pride—to Jesus. But how did Jesus respond to John's humility? It wasn't to humiliate him; instead, Jesus simply answered John: "Don't stop him . . . because there is no one who will perform a miracle in my name who can soon afterward speak evil of me. For whoever is not against us is for us. And whoever gives you a cup of water to drink in my name, because you belong to Christ—truly I tell you, he will never lose his reward" (vv. 39–41).

Jesus graciously taught John that, as a leader in His movement, John couldn't become prideful. He had to remain humble and pray. That's what leaders in Jesus' movement do.

Having a humble heart before the Lord does not mean you never walk in the darkness; having a humble heart means that when you do walk in darkness, you'll be quick to confess your sin and return to the light.

CHAPTER 18

WHAT'S SO AMAZING ABOUT GRACE?

Remember earlier when I explained that part III terrifies me? Well, it still does. As this chapter unfolds, keep in mind that it is not about our salvation. It is not about how someone is saved. It is not about whether someone is saved. Rather, it is about a relationship with God once we have *become* a Christian, and right before our eyes, John is readjusting how we understand this relationship. For the disciple Jesus loved, walking in the light is achieved one of two ways.

The first way is that you walk in the light as a result of your obedience to the Lord, which is the most desirable way to walk in the light as we embody the life of Christ (1 John 4:9). For example: "We [Christians] are his workmanship, created in Christ Jesus for good works, which God prepared ahead of time for us to do" (Eph. 2:10).

However, there is another way. Because we have sinned—and let's be honest, we still sin—the dark reality is that we are not able to walk in the light as much as we would hope. But there's good news. There's still a way to get back to the light. This is accomplished through prayer and the confession of your sin.

The questions are: Are you humble enough to admit you've sinned? Are you humble enough to admit you still sin?

Then the question becomes: Are you humble enough to confess that sin to God?

If you are, "he is faithful and righteous to forgive us our sins and to cleanse us from all unrighteousness" (1 John 1:9), which means the only reason unrighteousness would remain is if it is left unconfessed. And for our present purposes, being cleansed from unrighteousness is another way of saying you're walking in the light again.

In summary, in light of our fallen, sinful nature, John, through Jesus, has told us about another way in which a relationship with God is still possible. And these are the key ingredients: grace, humility, and prayer.

Now, I'm completely aware that John's teaching here could be potentially very dangerous left in the hands of some. I can hear it now: "Wait, so does this mean I can just go live however I want, and then all I have to do is confess my sin?"

[Sigh.] Of course not!

Or, maybe we are legitimately concerned with the message this might communicate, that sin isn't so bad because God will just forgive you.

However, literally right after John teaches us about confessing our sins and being cleansed from unrighteousness (1 John 1:9), he then says, "My little children, I am writing you these things so that you *may not* sin. But if anyone *does* sin, we have

an advocate with the Father—Jesus Christ the righteous one"
(1 John 2:1, emphasis mine).

The objective is not to sin, nor is it to promote sin, nor is to
diminish the severity of sin. The heart of the matter is that God,
in His grace, has designed a way for us as sinners to return to the
light when we do sin.

This is one of the most powerful and scary realities about
grace: God didn't design grace to be abused, but He did design
grace to withstand abuse and to defeat abuse. Yes, grace was
designed to offer forgiveness from sin, which would otherwise
prevent us from having an eternal relationship with God in
heaven. But grace also provides the means for Christians to have
a relationship with God here and now.

Like today. And tomorrow. And the next day.

If a Christian is to walk in the light, this is most fittingly
accomplished through obedience so that God's grace is not
abused. However, when that same Christian walks in darkness
due to sin, God has graciously provided a way for the Christian
to return to the light. But in order to return to the light, God
needs to cleanse them, and when God forgives someone, He
extends grace to them. He cleanses them. He brings them back
to the light.

Another way to think about this is that God lets you abuse
His grace as He offers to you more and more forgiveness.

This is why grace is so amazing.

I think Moses and Pharaoh provided a helpful illustration
of what it might look like for God to design grace to withstand
abuse.

The setting for this story is the looming first Passover, when
God dramatically and miraculously freed the Israelites from

Pharaoh in Egypt. In the Bible we find this story in the better part of the first fifteen chapters of Exodus. In the lead-up
to Pharaoh finally letting the people go, there was a series of
plagues, each sent by God so that Pharaoh would let the people go, so that the Israelites might worship God in the land He
promised they would live in.

For our purposes, I specifically want to look at those
instances when Moses prayed to God on behalf of Pharaoh,
because in those moments we really get to see what's so amazing
about grace.

The first plague didn't faze Pharaoh much at all. In this
plague, the Nile River was turned into blood while Pharaoh
bathed in it. Apparently, bathing in blood wasn't odd to Pharaoh
(Exod. 7:23).

In the second plague God sent frogs. Lots of frogs. The Bible
describes it as "heaps" of frogs (8:14).

This plague bothered Pharaoh a little more. We know this
because he asked Moses to pray to the Lord on his behalf that
the frogs would leave. In return, Pharaoh told Moses: "I will let
the people go and they can sacrifice to the LORD" (v. 8).

Moses listened and prayed to the Lord on behalf of Pharaoh,
then God answered Pharaoh's prayer, and the frogs died. The
Bible says, "There was a terrible odor in the land" (v. 14).
However, once Pharaoh saw that the problem with the frogs was
over, he went back on his word and didn't let the people go
(v. 15).

Stop for a moment.

Do you think that Moses knew Pharaoh was going to lie and
go back on his word? That's a hard question. I don't know.

What about God? Do you think He knew that Pharaoh was going to lie and go back on his word? Of course He knew Pharaoh would lie. He's God. He knows *everything*.

Yet God still graciously answers Pharaoh's prayer and gives him exactly what he wants.

That's God allowing grace to be abused.

Something similar happens with the fourth plague. This time it was flies: "And the LORD did this. Thick swarms of flies went into Pharaoh's palace and his officials' houses. Throughout Egypt the land was ruined because of the swarms of flies" (v. 24).

Again, Pharaoh asked Moses to pray to the Lord on his behalf. Moses even described the prayer request as a plea for help (v. 28). Moses then left Pharaoh and went out into the wilderness to pray for him (v. 30). Again, God answered Pharaoh's prayer, and the flies disappeared. Not one was left, the Bible says. Yet again, once Pharaoh got what he wanted from the Lord, he went back on his word and did not let the people go (vv. 31–32).

I have to ask again: Do you think God knew that Pharaoh would lie and not let the people go? Of course God knew this. He still knows everything. Yet again, He answered Pharaoh's prayer.

To say this another way: God knew this, and yet graciously, He permitted prayer to be abused.

Then there was the seventh plague, which was hail, unlike anything the world had ever seen. This hail was so bad that fire flashed in the midst of it (9:24). This plague really got Pharaoh's attention. He called for Moses and said: "I have sinned this time. . . . The LORD is the righteous one, and I and my people are the guilty ones. Make an appeal to the LORD. There has been enough of God's thunder and hail. I will let you go; you don't need to stay any longer" (vv. 27–28).

Could this be it? Could Pharaoh really have been turning to the Lord and admitting he's a sinner? That he was in the wrong? That his people were in the wrong?

It's really interesting here, because before Moses went out of the city to pray for Pharaoh, he first told Pharaoh what was going to happen. Moses described that he would stretch out his hands to the Lord, and when he did so the thunder would cease and there would be no more hail. This was to demonstrate to Pharaoh that the earth was the Lord's (v. 29). Moses also told Pharaoh that he knew that Pharaoh does not yet fear the Lord (v. 30).

If there was ever a time for Moses to refuse to pray for Pharaoh, this would seem like a good time. If there was ever a time for God not to answer Pharaoh's prayer, this would seem like a good time.

Yet, Moses' response to Pharaoh was to graciously pray again on Pharaoh's behalf. In addition, God's response to Pharaoh was to graciously answer his prayer request, and the rain and hail and thunder stopped. And when Pharaoh saw that the weather had changed, he sinned again and did not let the people go (v. 34).

Then there was an eighth plague, and guess what—it was just like the second, fourth, and seventh plagues.

The eighth plague was locusts, and there were so many that the people couldn't even see the land. They ate all that was left after the hail. The Bible describes how the locusts even covered and filled all the houses of the Egyptians.

And again, Pharaoh pled with Moses to pray to the Lord on his behalf. And again, he asked forgiveness for his sins. And again, Moses prayed on behalf of Pharaoh to the Lord. And again, the Lord answered Pharaoh's prayer by sending a strong west wind, which lifted and drove the locusts into the Red Sea. The Bible says: "Not a single locust was left in all the territory of Egypt" (Exod. 10:19). And again, once Pharaoh saw the locusts were gone, he refused to let the people go.

At the end of these series of plagues, before the Passover, do you know what God's biggest complaint to Pharaoh was?

It wasn't that he mistreated Moses by lying to him. It wasn't that he lied to God. It wasn't that he abused grace. It wasn't that he abused prayer—and not just any prayer. Don't forget, God answered *every one* of Pharaoh's prayers.

God's biggest complaint was Pharaoh's stubbornness, his unwillingness to humble himself before the Lord (v. 3).

God didn't design grace to be abused, but He did design grace to withstand and defeat abuse. In this instance, it was through prayer that God allowed His grace to be abused—over and over and over and over again—with the hope that Pharaoh would humble himself before the Lord.

> God's biggest complaint was Pharaoh's stubbornness, his unwillingness to humble himself before the Lord.

Believing that grace was designed to withstand abuse does not mean that Christians have a free pass to go and live however they'd like. Not at all. Again, that's why even after John explained how we can cleanse ourselves and walk in the light through the confession of our sins, he still begged them: "I am writing you these things so that you may not sin" (1 John 2:1).

But will some still read this and take advantage of God's grace? Sadly, yes.

Will some still assume that's what I'm *really* saying? Probably.

That's okay, though. I'm willing to take the chance.

Here's why.

Because when grace is understood this way, it provides the necessary spiritual space to fail graciously.

This is probably for another book, but I think much of where Christianity finds itself today is the result of a religion that does not afford people the ability to mess up or, even worse, fail. Instead, it has encouraged this strange version of hypocrisy clothed in authenticity, so that we become obsessed with looking like we've got it all together—or just enough of it together. (After all, if we looked *perfect*, we would no longer look *perfectly authentic*, would we?)

It is not surprising that this version of Christianity does not worry itself with being humble or confessing its sin. Failure is necessary, though, if we are to develop and grow as Christians.

I would even say that as Christians, if we don't allow for the sacred space of failure, we are not truly conforming people (or ourselves) to the image of Christ. That's not because Christ was a failure; it's because if we are to become more like Jesus and less like ourselves, then we must *become* less sinful.

Notice what I didn't say. I didn't say, "If we are to become more like Jesus and less like ourselves, then we must *appear* less sinful."

As it exists now, the paradigm for walking in the light is simple, because it is measured almost solely by what can be seen. Thus, the paradigm is that you either fail—which is marked by poor behavior—or you succeed, which is evidenced by your obedience. In other words, you did the right thing. "Well done, good and faithful servant" (Matt. 25:21).

However, I think the paradigm needs to change. Life is more complex; it needs to live up to amazing grace.

So, what would a different paradigm look like for walking in the light? I think Christians can deepen in their relationship with God in two ways.

For starters, I think walking in the dark would still be associated with sin, but what would be most troubling in this new paradigm is that sinful behavior is done from a prideful heart. "Prideful heart" here means that although God has permitted grace to be abused, the Christian would rather attempt to remedy sin on their own. This typically looks like pridefully trying to clean up their sin so as to not commit that sin any longer. As if that fixes the problem.

This is the kind of heart that has a self-sufficient attitude. But even with their best attempts, they have never really dealt with the unrighteousness in their life. Even if they have successfully treated the sin, they still have unrighteousness that remains.

Why?

Because correcting one's behavior or attitude toward sin doesn't cleanse one of unrighteousness. Only the blood of Christ is able to cleanse the Christian from sin (1 John 1:7). Thus, the combination of sinful behavior and a prideful heart prevents one from walking in the light and living in a close relationship with God.

Walking in the light in our new paradigm would still be measured by one's obedience. This blend of obedience and a humble heart is relationally the most loving response to God as we obey Him out of our love for Him and others. What's also important is that in this new paradigm would be a sense of safety and security because the Christian would now be able to admit that obedience is difficult when the standard is Christ, who is perfect.

The Christian would no longer feel any pressure to have it all together. Why? Because there is also a second way to walk in the light in this new paradigm.

It goes like this: walking in the light is somehow associated with sinful behavior.

Wait, what?

Yes, sinful behavior.

The reality is, you will mess up. You are only fooling yourself if you think avoiding sin is possible (1 John 1:8, 10). But what's different this time is that you have a humble heart. Thus, sinful behavior plus a humble heart leads the Christian back into the light.

But what's a humble heart? A humble heart means a heart that confesses sin and, in so doing, is cleansed from all unrighteousness, thereby restoring a person to the light (1 John 1:9).

What is so amazing about God is that He has graciously provided a way to have a relationship with Him in the midst of our sinfulness.

This is what's so amazing about grace—that God has designed it to withstand confession of sin over and over again so that He can have a relationship with humans.

This is walking in the light.

CHAPTER 19

DO YOU HEAR IT?

There is a story in the Gospel of John of a woman caught early in the morning cheating on her husband.

Later that same day Jesus was in the temple, and the people were grabbing their seats, getting ready to listen to Him teach (John 8:2). Once everyone was settled in, the scribes and Pharisees, in the middle of temple, with all the people looking on, brought this woman before Jesus.

I bet some people today avoid going to church for this very reason, because they are so afraid they will be found out. And, of course, they think when that happens, someone will bring them to the pastor in front of the whole congregation.

Then the scribes and Pharisees told Jesus, in front of all the people, that this woman was just caught having sex with another man.

How humiliating.

This woman had to feel so ashamed in the hands of these religious men. The scribes and Pharisees didn't care—they wanted to catch Jesus teaching something wrong so they could have a charge to bring against Him.

In the law, it was commanded by Moses to stone a woman caught in adultery. But what was Jesus' response going to be? If it was anything different than what Moses said, then they'd got Him.

But Jesus did this strange thing. He bent down and started to write with His finger on the ground. The Bible doesn't tell us what He wrote, though. It just says: "Jesus stooped down and started writing on the ground with his finger" (v. 6).

Then the biblical account describes how Jesus stood up and told the Scribes and Pharisees, "The one without sin among you should be the first to throw a stone at her" (v. 7). Then Jesus bent back down and started to write again with His finger on the ground.

What was He writing? I don't know.

I have a guess, though. What if He was calling them adulterers? What if Jesus was accusing them of the same sin? Take a look at the first three chapters of Jeremiah, and let me know what you think.

Anyway, the Bible next describes the scene like this: "*When they heard this*, they left one by one, starting with the older men. Only he was left, with the woman standing in the center" (v. 9).

The Bible describes it this way: "When they heard this." Heard what?

It couldn't have been that they merely heard Jesus say, "The one without sin among you should be the first to throw a stone at her" (v. 7a). Why? That seems logical. But it was after Jesus writes on the ground that the Bible says they heard it. Not after

He said, "The one without sin among you should be the first to throw a stone at her" (v. 7b).

In this very short story, John actually takes the time to describe this twice—that twice Jesus bent down to write with His finger on the ground.

So what did they hear? I think they heard the Holy Spirit, and as a result, one by one, they began to walk away "starting with the older men" (v. 9a).

As Jesus was left standing with the woman, in the midst of all the people listening on, He asked her a question: "Woman, where are they? Has no one condemned you?" (v. 10).

Remember, this was in front of everyone.

The woman said, "No one, Lord" (v. 11a). And Jesus said, "Neither do I condemn you. . . . Go, and from now on do not sin anymore" (v. 11b).

The original intent of the scribes and Pharisees was to shame this woman and trick Jesus into teaching something so erroneous that they might have a charge to bring against Him and prevent His movement (Christianity) from going any further.

Notice the difference between Jesus and the scribes and Pharisees in their responses to someone caught sinning. In the middle of the temple, with all the people there, the scribes and Pharisees made known this woman's sin. They humiliated her. Yet Jesus quietly bent down and wrote on the ground (twice), exposing not her sin, but their sin. Not with words, but within their hearts.

It was like Jesus didn't need to say anything; the scribes and Pharisees knew in their hearts that they were sinners. From the outside, they wanted others to think they weren't sinners. But because they were, they couldn't throw a stone at her.

The whole assembly heard what this woman did, thanks to the scribes and Pharisees. But God revealed their sin to them privately, in such a way that they "heard this" (v. 9), even though no words were spoken.

God deals graciously with sinners.

Even to the scribes and Pharisees, who should have been put to shame, just like they did to the woman.

Have you ever noticed that Jesus was always gracious, particularly with women caught in adultery? I can't help but think that when He interacted with this woman caught in adultery, He saw a little of His mom in her.

There had to be some people who never believed Mary's story. They never believed that the angel Gabriel visited this virgin and told her she would soon become pregnant by the work of the Holy Spirit (Luke 1:26–38). Surely not everyone believed her, that she would soon give birth to the Son of God. Surely some even called her an adulterous woman and accused her of cheating on Joseph.

Jesus loved His mom, and He had a soft spot for this woman too.

Let's get back to John 8:9: "When they heard this, they left one by one, starting with the older men. Only he was left, with the woman in the center."

The Bible describes that they heard something. What did they hear? They heard their hearts.

Let me describe what they heard theologically.

What the scribes and Pharisees heard was the convicting work of the Spirit of God in their lives. They were made aware of their sin, and because they were now aware of their sin, they had to drop the stones clenched in their hands and walk away.

That's why Jesus said, "The one without sin among you should be the first to throw a stone at her" (v. 7).

Have you ever "heard this" before?

Later in the Gospel of John we find Jesus preparing the disciples for what was about to happen. Jesus would be handed over to the authorities and in short time be put to death on the cross—a humiliating death in front of everyone.

In order to prepare the disciples, Jesus told them that He was sending a Helper. The Helper was the Holy Spirit. The Helper was going to bear witness about Jesus and all the things Jesus had said to them so that they would be kept from "stumbling" (John 16:1). Jesus even said it is to the disciples' advantage that He go away, because if Jesus stayed, then the Helper wouldn't come (v. 7).

Another way to understand that the disciples would be kept from "stumbling" would be to say that the Holy Spirit was going to help keep the disciples walking in the light (1 John 1:5–7).

How is the Holy Spirit going to do this, though? Jesus said, "When he [Holy Spirit] comes, he will *convict* the world about sin, righteousness, and judgment" (John 16:8, emphasis mine).

Convict?

Yes, convict.

I can hear you now. "Part III is super fun and encouraging. We are talking about how sinful we are, that we need to confess our sin to God, and how the Holy Spirit makes us feel bad when we sin."

Hang in there with me.

The Holy Spirit convicts the world of sin.

What does *conviction* mean? It means that the Holy Spirit has examined your sin carefully. It means that the Holy Spirit has exposed your sin. It means that the Holy Spirit has brought you to a point at which you now recognize you are doing something wrong. It means that the Holy Spirit has brought to light your sin.

It means you've "heard this."

God reveals (convicts), and we respond (confess). This is prayer at its holiest. This is when prayer makes you holy.

This is a common lament: "Why don't I ever hear God speak to me?" or "I don't ever hear from God."

Let's unpack this a little.

What if we really believed that God already knows our sin? (Like we read in 1 John 1:8 and 1 John 1:10.) What if we really believed that God, not *might*, will cleanse us of all unrighteousness if we confess our sins? (Like we read in 1 John 1:9.) What if all that was required is a humble heart to go before God and confess our sin? What if this wasn't humiliating at all?

God never responds to our humility with humiliation. The woman caught in adultery is a helpful example of this.

Confession is God's means of providing an actual way for us to return to Him, even as sinners.

To walk in the light, as John describes it.

What if we also started to look at the convicting work of the Holy Spirit, not as a humiliating experience with God where He shames us because of our sin, but as a gentle invitation from the Spirit to restore our relationship with God? What if conviction from the Holy Spirit was one of the most beautiful things we've ever heard from God, because it demonstrates that, in spite of our sin, He wants a relationship with us, and there is something terrible in the way?

Have you ever wondered why almost immediately after you sin you feel convicted?

You feel bad. You know you've done something wrong. And that feeling happens almost immediately.

The scribes and Pharisees felt it too, but the biblical text says they "heard this" (John 8:9).

I don't think God is just waiting for you to fail and mess up because He wants to be the first to tell you. Instead, He doesn't want a moment to pass whereby His relationship with you is in a bad place, so He immediately presses in on you with the hope that you will return to Him. That's how much God loves you.

> Confession is God's means of providing an actual way for us to return to Him.

He wants you to come home, like the prodigal son. That son returned in shame, but the father wouldn't let him live in shame. The father, instead, threw a feast because he loved his son (Luke 15:11–32).

And remember—there will always be those siblings who will be mad that the father doesn't shame you. But that's their problem, not yours.

So next time you hear this and are convicted, please know that God is calling you home. He loves you.

Now, you might be asking the question: "But what do I do with those feelings of shame?" I think they're from Satan. Let me explain.

Here is the great difficulty with the feeling of conviction. It's a complicated feeling. When someone feels the convicting work of the Holy Spirit, it can also feel just like shame. As a result, we often don't try to distinguish between the two feelings and, instead, just assume that they are one and the same. But they're not.

When you feel conviction, that is from the Holy Spirit. When you feel shame, that is from the devil. How do you know the difference?

Everything about the ministry of conviction is meant to drive you back into a relationship with God through prayer.

Shame does the complete opposite of conviction.

Shame drives you away from a relationship with God. Shame drives you away from prayer. Shame attempts to keep you in darkness.

If conviction exposes your sin so that you might confess it, shame exposes your sin and tells you God will never forgive you for that. If conviction brings to light your sin, shame tempts you into thinking God wants you to stay away and not bring that sin into His precious, pure, and holy light.

When sin is brought to light and you feel the desire to run away from God, feel the desire not to confess, feel like God doesn't want a relationship with you, feel like God won't forgive you for that sin, *that is not from God.* God's grace was designed for forgiveness.

The Bible has a few verses that cast light on the difficulty in determining if we are feeling something from God or the devil. In his letter to the church in Ephesus, Paul writes, "For our struggle is not against flesh and blood, but against the rulers, against the authorities, against the cosmic powers of this darkness, against evil, spiritual forces in the heavens" (Eph. 6:12).

It takes spiritual effort to distinguish between conviction and shame because rulers, authorities, forces of evil, and cosmic powers are all attempting to wrestle you away from the pursuit of the Holy Spirit, who wants to bring you out of darkness and back into the light.

And yet this magnificent battle is taking place deep within us as we ponder what to do after we sin. A feeling as familiar to us as our best friend.

In another letter, but to a different church, Paul writes, "For Satan disguises himself as an angel of light. So it is no great surprise if his servants also disguise themselves as servants of righteousness" (2 Cor. 11:14–15).

I think some of the brilliant work of Satan is to take the emotion or experience or sound of the convicting ministry of the Holy Spirit and pervert it so that one feels and experiences and hears shame. The Holy Spirit attempts to draw us back into a relationship with God; the devil, appearing as an angel of light, tries to push us away, as far away as he can, from a relationship with God.

Back to our lament from earlier about never hearing from God. Maybe you do hear from God. Maybe you hear from God a lot—like, every day. Maybe you had no idea God spoke to you this much. To put it another way, maybe "the angel of light" (2 Cor. 11:14) was disguising God's voice as shame.

And what about those who are not Christians? The Bible also says that the Holy Spirit convicts them as well.

In the church of my youth, this was often taught to mean something like God is pointing His finger at non-Christians and saying, "You're a sinner." Or it was explained that there won't be an excuse as to why a non-Christian is going to hell, because look, God was convicting them of sin, and they didn't respond to it. Often, those who taught this would quote John 16:8 as

their proof text: "When he [the Holy Spirit] comes, he will convict the world about sin, righteousness, and judgment."

In many ways this verse was used to justify the reality that
God loves humanity, although many will not be going to heaven.
In other words, it isn't God's fault.

What if we understood that God isn't guilting people into
confession? Instead, what if the conviction from the Holy Spirit
upon nonbelievers was really the birth pains of a relationship
God so desires with one of His children?

The Holy Spirit isn't shaming nonbelievers; rather, the Holy
Spirit desires nonbelievers to become believers. The Holy Spirit
is trying to get their attention. Not just so that they are "saved,"
but because He wants a relationship.

If the intent is to share the gospel (good news) with someone
who doesn't believe, it seems as though it would be far greater
news to share that God desires a relationship with them instead
of scaring our non-Christian friends into believing in Jesus with
a certain theology of conviction.

What about Satan?

Seriously, Kyle? Satan again?

If the "angel of light" (2 Cor. 11:14) attempts to deceive the
Christian into thinking that conviction and shame are one and
the same, what do you think he will do with those who do not
believe?

If the convicting work of the Holy Spirit upon nonbelievers
is the labor pains of a relationship God desires with His children, it makes perfect sense that Satan would want to take this
work of the Spirit and pervert it into the abhorrent emotion of
shame.

How many times have you heard a non-Christian say something like, "God could never love me," "You have no idea what I've done," or "Trust me, God wants nothing to do with me"? Many non-Christians have given up on a possible relationship with God because they have believed Satan, not the Holy Spirit.

But are they really rejecting God? Or are they rejecting a false idea about God?

What if they weren't responding to the Holy Spirit's conviction because Satan has so twisted that emotion to the point that the non-Christian just feels satanic shame? And based on this shame, they don't want to believe in God.

Honestly, I wouldn't either.

What if Satan has so deceived non-Christians that they have missed the beauty in the pursuit of the Holy Spirit, where the Holy Spirit draws non-Christians to turn their hearts to God through the conviction of their sin?

As Christians we need to reclaim this story and communicate that God doesn't shame our unbelieving friends, that the devil is up to no good. Instead, God convicts them of sin because He loves them and wants a relationship with them. The Holy Spirit convicts them so that they might hear this and find out what's so amazing about grace.

PART IV

CONFESS YOUR SINS TO ONE ANOTHER

(A STUDY IN JAMES)

If confession of sin ends with sorrow,
it hasn't gone far enough.
Confessing sin is an opportunity to rejoice in the gospel.
—Catherine Parks

INTRODUCTION
TO PART IV

John's desire is that a Christian would confess their sin to God so that they might return to walking in the light.

Over the next three chapters, we are going to see that James wants Christians to confess their sin to one another, which is a little different from John.

At some point I think you are going to ask: "Well, which one is it? Am I supposed to confess to God or to someone else?" And I think we're going to find that James actually agrees with John, but he has his own way of explaining it. James is going to talk a lot about the prayer of faith.

My hope is that we will come to find that, for James, the command that one should confess to another is simply an outward manifestation of someone who has already confessed their sin to God.

In other words, confessing your sins to one another has more to do with confessing your sins to God than it does with confessing to another person.

CHAPTER 20

THE PRAYER OF WHAT?

Did you know Jesus had brothers? And sisters too? He may have actually come from a big family.

The Gospel of Matthew includes a scene in which Jesus returns to Nazareth, His hometown. While home, Jesus taught at His synagogue. He must have performed some miracles too, because the Bible describes the reaction of the people toward Jesus as "astonished." They asked themselves: "Where did this man get this wisdom and these miraculous powers?" (Matt. 13:54).

In other words, Isn't this Jesus, the little kid we saw and knew growing up? You know, the carpenter's son, and Mary was His mother, with her somewhat complicated past. Wasn't Jesus the oldest of many brothers and sisters? (vv. 55–56).

One of His younger brothers was named James, who would later become a key figure in the early church. James was a righteous man, so much so that he was given the moniker "James the Just." He was a leader of the church in Jerusalem

(Acts 15), and the Bible also tells us that James was an apostle as well (Gal. 1:19).

James held to the same theological foundation as John, the disciple Jesus loved. For James and John, what was most important in the Christian life was to focus on loving God (James 1:12) and your neighbor (James 2:8). For them, this was the greatest commandment. This truth to live by was not something James made up; it was something he learned from his older brother (Matt. 22:34–40).

And just like John, James taught a lot about prayer. Not just any kind of prayer, but like John, he writes a lot about confession. Apparently, James' reputation wasn't just as a righteous man, but he was also known as a man of prayer.

I wonder, though, if he was known as a righteous man, not because he always did the right thing, but rather, because he prayed so much. And not just any kind of prayer, but because he confessed his sin so much.

One church historian named Eusebius (c. 260–340) is commonly referred to as "the father of church history," and he actually records some of James' prayer habits. Eusebius writes:

> And he [James] was in the habit of entering alone into the temple, and was frequently found upon his knees begging forgiveness for the people, so that his knees became hard like those of a camel, in consequence of his constantly bending them in his worship of God, and asking forgiveness for the people.

This wasn't a man who just told you he'd be praying for you. He wasn't a man who merely taught about the importance of prayer. He was a doer of prayer.

Doer?

Yeah, a doer.

I'll explain more in a moment.

There was a difference between John and James, though. Where John talked a lot about confession and walking in the light, James focused on what he called the *prayer of faith*.

What's important to remember is that when James talked about prayer or confession, it must be understood within the context of love. Just like John.

Not shame, but conviction. Not prideful, but humble. Not darkness, but light. Not weak prayer, but strong. Not dirty, but clean. Not at a distance, but in a relationship.

Here is what I'd like to do. Just like we did with 2 Chronicles earlier, we are going to start at the end of the letter and work back to the beginning.

In his very last chapter (chapter 5), James talks about the importance of prayer and particularly the prayer of faith. It goes like this:

> Is anyone among you suffering? He should pray. Is anyone cheerful? He should sing praises. Is anyone among you sick? He should call for the elders of the church, and they are to pray over him, anointing him with oil in the name of the Lord. *The prayer of faith* will save the sick person, and the Lord will raise him up; if he has committed sins, he will be forgiven. (James 5:13–15, emphasis mine)

James says a few different things about prayer here. He talks about righteous prayer, healing prayer, and the prayer of faith. Throughout the next few chapters, we will devote our attention to these verses so that we might think more theologically together about all this.

But for now, here is the question: What is the prayer of faith? After James writes verses 13 through 15, the whole letter has only five verses left. So it isn't like he has all this time to unpack what these verses mean. And just prior to verses 13 through 15, James warns about the dangers of wealth, taming the tongue, and showing partiality in the church.

So what's going on?

Well, let's peek at the beginning of the letter to see if he has anything else to say about prayer. Hint: he does.

James opens his letter talking about how Christians experience all kinds of trials (James 1:2). What's a trial? As it relates to one's spirituality, a trial is something that reveals the nature or character of one's faith.

For James, it's essential to understand that when you experience a trial, there is a difference between being tested or tempted. Why? Because being able to distinguish between a test or temptation might be the very difference between whether you'll continue to love God in the midst of the trial.

For James, God tests a Christian's faith, and when a Christian loves God throughout the test, it produces a spiritual steadfastness (vv. 3, 12). A steadfastness that, in its full effect, leaves the Christian lacking in nothing (v. 4).

On the other hand, a common way that one is tempted is to become lured and enticed by one's own desires. And for James, a great example of something that tempts us is wealth. God doesn't hate wealth, and neither does James, but the difficulty with wealth is that it provides the means for Christians to generate their own will and mistake it for God's.

That is why James says: "Let the brother of humble circumstances boast in his exaltation, but let the rich boast in his humiliation because he will pass away like a flower of the field. For the sun rises and, together with the scorching wind, dries up the grass; its flower falls off, and its beautiful appearance perishes. In the same way, the rich person will wither away while pursuing his activities" (vv. 9–11).

Okay, James, we get it. But how are you, as a Christian, able to understand if you are being tested or if you are being lured by your own desires?

Pray.

Pray so much that your knees become like the knees of a camel.

James says we should pray and ask God for wisdom to be able to tell the difference (v. 5). Let God reveal to you if you are being tested or if you are being tempted by your own desires.

James even uses similar "light" language that John used earlier, describing the "Father of lights" as only giving good and perfect gifts (vv. 16–18). In other words, those seeking to know the difference need not worry; God will illuminate the answer. It's what He does. It's who He is. He is light.

This isn't easy, though, and you need to be willing to check your heart in the process, because the heart can be very deceiving. It can trick you into thinking you aren't being driven by your own desires when, in reality, you are.

However, it's worth it to pray this way, to allow yourself to be vulnerable, to allow God to reveal the kind of heart that is producing your prayers, because the One examining your heart is gracious and merciful.

James promises that God won't even hesitate or give it a second thought. He'll immediately answer the prayers of the one who humbly prays, seeking wisdom.

God is even said to give "generously" in His answer to this kind of humble prayer (v. 5).

However, the one who prays from a heart that is used to getting its own desires will not experience God's abundance. In fact, James says this kind of prayer will be discouraging and cast doubt on the one praying (v. 6), because this person should not expect to receive anything from the Lord" (v. 7).

Why is it so important to know the difference between being tested or tempted?

Not *if* but *when* you experience a trial of some kind in your life, if you don't know the difference, you might find yourself doubting God instead of seeking refuge and comfort in the Father of Lights. And here's the thing: the only way you will know the difference is by humbly seeking God in prayer. When you try to figure out if you are being tested or tempted based on your own wisdom, based on your own riches, you are as good as a flower withering in the heat without water (v. 11). Or a sailboat being tossed and driven by the wind as it's lost at sea (v. 6).

I've often heard James 1:19 preached as a Christian version of a self-help tip. It says: "My dear brothers and sisters, understand this: Everyone should be quick to listen, slow to speak, and slow to anger." And so, as Christians, we try to do the "Christianly" thing and listen more and talk less as a way that we might love one another—which isn't a bad thing at all.

However, reading this verse that way has often led to an interpretation that has more to do with a human communicating to another human, as though this verse is meant to enhance our interpersonal communication skills.

Let's offer another interpretation of this verse, shall we? A prayerful interpretation because, after all, isn't that what James has been talking about so far in the opening eighteen verses?

It says first to "be quick to listen." Listen to what? Listen to another human? Listen to the music? Listen to the wind?

No.

The person is praying. Talking to God. Asking God for wisdom.

Maybe "listen" is in reference to listening in prayer.

In verse 5, James tells us to pray and ask for something. That if anyone is lacking in wisdom, specifically about a trial in their life, they should pray. This means God's wisdom enables you to have the capacity to understand a trial in your life.

Notice that doesn't mean the trial will go away or that God will magically fix all your problems. Instead, God wants to show you how the trial is not what you think it is. It's not a temptation. It's a test.

Then, after you pray for God's wisdom, it is best to listen and not get in the way by speaking. Because when you speak, your own desires distract you. They tempt you, which is why verse 19 then says to be "slow to speak."

The more you speak, the more you start to believe yourself and stop listening for God's reply. It's as though you are lured and enticed by your own desires.

What if by being "slow to speak" James means you are protecting yourself from your own desires so that you won't miss when God reveals His wisdom?

It takes humility to pray and ask for help. It also takes humility to pray and then be quiet before the Lord—not offering your own wisdom, but rather waiting for God's wisdom.

And what if being "slow to anger" means you are humble enough to listen when God answers your prayer and provides the needed wisdom during the trial—even if that wisdom is different than what you had hoped for?

> It takes humility to pray and ask for help.

An angry person is one who gets frustrated that God isn't adapting His wisdom to meet his or her desires.

What if being "slow to anger" also means that the one praying does not get angry when God reveals the kind of heart you have in prayer? In other words, when God reveals that you have, in fact, been tricked by your own desires, you don't get mad.

I think James 1:19 has more to do with how we pray than it does with how we should speak to each other. It's a verse in which the brother of Jesus teaches us how to ask God for wisdom in the midst of a trial.

James then talks about not just being a listener of the Word, but also a doer of the Word, not just a talker about the Word, but one who actually lives out what the Word says (v. 22).

It would be like a person who does not merely talk a lot about prayer, but actually embodies prayer, so much so that his or her knees become like that of a camel.

When Christians' words do not match their lives, they become visible manifestations of a worthless religion on display for the world to see (v. 26). Yet religion that is pure and undefiled is this: "To look after orphans and widows in their distress and to keep oneself unstained from the world" (v. 27).

This verse seems to change the direction of the first chapter. James has spent all this time talking about prayer, and now he is talking about visiting orphans and widows. But I don't think James changed his mind or got sidetracked. Instead, I think his theology of prayer is developing right before our eyes. In addition to prayer, the kind of life one lives exposes the kind of heart a person has.

The sequence of events seems to be that one is to pray and seek God's wisdom (v. 5). Then one is to be quiet and listen (v. 19). But that doesn't mean that just because one is quietly listening one is to sit idly by and wait for God to answer prayer. James 1:19 doesn't read: "Let every person be quick to hear, slow to speak, slow to anger, slow to action." Despite what some people seem to think, prayer is not the enemy of action.

That would be selfish and self-serving. Inaction provides far too much time for your heart to tempt you and get in the way of what wisdom God is trying to reveal to you. Instead, in a posture of prayer, we are called to quietly love our neighbors. To love the widows and orphans (v. 27). In other words, to serve one another.

And for James, somewhere in-between prayer and being a doer of the Word, something supernatural takes place.

God's wisdom, which was previously mysterious, now is revealed. God's wisdom, which was previously unknown, now is known. God's wisdom, which was previously confusing, now is understandable.

After James tells the Christian to be slow to anger in verse 19, he talks about how the Christian is to "put away all filthiness and rampant wickedness and receive with meekness the implanted word, which is able to save your souls" (v. 21 ESV). I even think this is a reference to prayer. Particularly, prayer of confession.

"Put away" in James 1:21 (ESV) means the same thing as "rid oneself." Thus, James tells us to rid ourselves of all filthiness and wickedness. Doesn't that sound a lot like "cleanse yourself"?

The opposite of being filthy is to be clean. How do you do that? Remember, according to 1 John 1:9, you confess your sin and you are "cleanse[d] from all unrighteousness." For James, when God reveals your anger, the response should be to confess that sin so that you might be cleansed.

Then James tells the Christian to be a doer of the Word, and not just a listener (vv. 22–23). He uses imagery of a mirror and says that the one who merely hears the word but doesn't live it out is like a man who looks at himself in the mirror, walks away, and forgets how sinful he is (vv. 24–25). For James, Christians should be different.

Christians should look not into the mirror, but rather into God's perfect law, the law of liberty, and persevere by being a doer who acts (v. 25a). In other words, in confession there is freedom from the filthiness and wickedness of sin.

This person, James says, "Will be blessed" (v. 25b).

The blessed man, who is a doer of the Word, does this: visits orphans and widows *and* keeps himself "unstained from the world" (v. 27).

Again, this sounds like John. There are two ways to walk in the light. Through obedience, which for James would be visiting the orphans and widows. But also, walking in the light looks like confessing your sins so that you can return to the light.

> In confession there is freedom from the filthiness and wickedness of sin.

James uses the language of being "unstained from the world" (v. 27). Again, this sounds like John. For one is unstained from the world as one is cleansed when confessing sin to God.

This topic of confession fits well, not just with 1 John, but with James too, who will further discuss the importance of confession in James 5.

By the time we get to James 4 there has already been some discussion surrounding two trials the church is going through, two conflicts that are causing fights. The first is that the church is showing partiality toward some (2:1–13). The second is that the church needs to watch how it speaks to one another (3:1–12).

Then in James 4:1 (ESV) he asks: "What causes quarrels and what causes fights among you?" I know two good places to start.

But James doesn't bring them up. Instead, he comments about this war that is being waged *within* (v. 1). Their conflicting passions are messing around with their ability to pray.

James writes: "You do not have, because you do not ask. You ask and do not receive, because you ask wrongly, to spend it on your passions" (vv. 2b–3 ESV). Thus, James begs them to humbly submit to God (vv. 6–7). And what exactly does that submission look like?

James writes, "Cleanse your hands, you sinners, and purify your hearts, you double-minded" (v. 8 ESV).

Translation: confess your sins, cleanse yourself from all remaining unrighteousness. (Sounds like 1 John 1:9, right?)

That is what submission looks like. And the only one who can prayerfully submit to the Lord is the one who is humble enough to admit to being a sinner.

Then in James 5 he addresses some people in the church who are suffering and sick. He says that if anyone is suffering, he or she should pray (v. 13). He says that if there is anyone who is sick, the elders of the church should pray over him or her (v. 14).

Then James says something interesting. He writes, "And the prayer of faith will save the one who is sick, and the Lord will raise him up. And if he has committed sins, he will be forgiven" (v. 15 ESV).

The prayer that saves the one who is sick, that brings forgiveness to the sinner, for James, is only the prayer of faith.

But how do I get the prayer of faith?

What if I told you that the answer is that we have to confess our sins to one another, that this is how you obtain the prayer of faith?

Doesn't that sound super fun?

You're probably saying right now, "I'm good. I'm not doing that. You can keep your prayer of faith."

CHAPTER 21

YOU GO FIRST

Have I convinced you yet that James has a serious interest in prayer? That maybe even his whole letter is about prayer? I hope so.

But not any kind of prayer will do. It has to be the prayer of faith. That is the most powerful kind of prayer.

But how do you start praying with the prayer of faith?

Is it some magical chant? Is it some particular word order that unlocks the mystery of this prayer? No.

Thankfully, James doesn't hide what the prayer of faith is, and he doesn't hide how to do it either. He tells us, but just because he tells us doesn't mean it will be easy to pray this way.

The very first word in James 5:16 is important if you want to know what the prayer of faith is. James writes, "Therefore." Therefore what?

"Therefore, confess your sins to one another and pray for one another, so that you may be healed. The prayer of a righteous person is very powerful in its effect" (5:16).

Why is "therefore" so important?

Because that word is James' way of saying, "Everything I just told you in verses 13 through 15 will work if you do verse 16!" In other words, everything we've just read in James 5:13–15 is going to find its logical conclusion in what comes after the "therefore."

And he's urging us to confess our sins to one another.

Remember James 5:13–15 and all the different references to prayer?

> Is anyone among you suffering? He should pray.
> Is anyone cheerful? He should sing praises. Is
> anyone among you sick? He should call for the
> elders of the church, and they are to pray over
> him, anointing him with oil in the name of the
> Lord. The prayer of faith will save the sick per-
> son, and the Lord will raise him up; if he has
> committed sins, he will be forgiven.

After reading these verses one might walk away thinking to themselves, *Well, what's the big deal?* Of course, when someone is suffering or sick, we Christians should pray with them and for them.

I bet there is a chance that this might be a little convicting, because so many Christians are accustomed to quickly say, "I'll be praying for you," when trouble arises, but they never really do. Instead, too often, we are quick to send a text, or flowers, or write a warm "thinking of you" note on social media, but we don't actually pray to God on someone's behalf.

However, that isn't even the kind of prayer James has in mind at this point. He specifically wants us to confess our sins to one another. When this happens, prayer becomes powerful. This kind of prayer makes things happen.

"Therefore, confess your sins to one another and pray for one another, so that you may be healed. *The prayer of a righteous person* is very powerful in its effect" (v. 16, emphasis mine).

But who is this righteous person James is talking about? The answer to this question is important because the righteous person is the one with great and powerful prayers.

According to 1 John 1:9, righteousness is achieved not only through obedience but through confession too: "If we confess our sins, he is faithful and righteous to forgive us our sins and to cleanse us from all unrighteousness."

I think this verse from 1 John helps us better understand when James writes, "Therefore, confess your sins to one another and pray for one another" (James 5:16). The one James has in mind is the one who is doing the praying, not the one being prayed for. James has in mind the doer of prayer.

In other words, he wants you to be a powerful man or woman of prayer and not merely a receiver of prayer. And it's not enough just to pray—he wants healed people to pray, righteous people to pray.

According to James, the way you get healed is by confessing your sins, which is exactly what John is saying. According to John, if you confess your sins, God will cleanse you (1 John 1:9). Please don't miss this. For John, what does God cleanse you from? *Unrighteousness.*

Thus, in order to get from unrighteousness to righteousness, we must confess our sins.

In order to get from dirty to clean, we must confess our sins.

In order to get from darkness to light, we must confess our sins.

And once sin is confessed, God forgives you and cleanses you, and you are healed.

Then James wants you to go and pray. You're healed. You're clean. You're forgiven. Your prayers are powerful, so use them. Don't hoard them. Now is the time to put them into action.

Humility is the only thing God demands from the one who is confessing sin. It takes humility to admit you're sick and need healing. It takes humility to admit you're walking in the darkness. It takes humility to admit your prayers are weak due to unrighteousness.

Prayer takes humility. But God never responds by humiliating us. He just doesn't. I refuse to let us forget this.

Not only is James instructing you on how you should pray in faith, but he is also shedding light on who you should have pray for you. You should no longer want just anyone merely to pray for you when you're sick or suffering. No way—you should want someone who confesses their sins (often!) to pray for you.

You should no longer want just any elder in the church praying for you; rather, you want the elder in the church praying over you that you know confesses their sins!

Why?

Because you want prayer that is powerful, right?

I mean, if you're sick, you do want to get healed, right?

And James tells us who in your church is the one with the most powerful prayers. It's not the one who looks like they have it all together. Nope. It's the one who confesses their sins.

The prayer of faith is prayed by righteous men and women. And the way a righteous person prays is by first confessing sins.

It still doesn't make it any more comfortable, this whole "confess your sins to one another" thing.

So why don't we like confessing our sins to each other? My first thought is (with a rather sarcastic smile on my face): "You go first."

I can still remember asking people to pray for me and my anger. It has taken the Lord many years for me to get a handle on not getting quickly frustrated. But I can still remember those friends who would listen to me confess this vulnerable and intimate experience I was going through. And once I was done, they would say something like, "Me too." "I can relate." "I know what you mean."

Then they would begin to confess to me their own sin, and it wasn't good either. I remember looking at them, with a little mixture of sadness and anger, thinking, *Why did you never say anything to me?* It was almost like someone needed to go first.

Confessing sin in your life can bring a kind of healing community once thought impossible. But it takes the humble leap of faith for someone to go first.

Being humble with other people will always be scary. You never know how they will respond. You never know if they will reject you, or maybe even worse, distance themselves from you. Many people prefer to surround themselves only with people who have it all together, and when you are humble, it's really hard to have it all together.

Sadly, too many churches have made it abundantly clear that they only want people to attend their church who have it all together. Those are shallow people. Those are dying churches. I don't think Jesus' brother would attend that church. I don't think the disciple Jesus loved would either.

What about this? Maybe if you really want to know if you've found a friend, humbly confess your sin to them. If they can handle it, you might have found someone worth walking through life with.

Or maybe you really want to know if you've found a good church? Humbly confess your sin to some people in the church. If they can handle it, you just might have found a good church.

But how do you know if they can handle it? Maybe they'll respond with, "Me too" or "I can relate."

> I'm over people and churches that can't handle the reality that people sin.

I don't know about you, but I'm over people and churches that can't handle the reality that people sin.

I'm also tired of friendships that come with the pressure of needing to have the perfect marriage, kids, job, family.

It's exhilarating and life-giving once you've found people who are willing to admit they don't have it all together, willing to confess they aren't perfect. Heck, they aren't even good.

Those are people I can relate to—the ones who are trying their best to love God and those around them, even if they don't always achieve it.

CHAPTER 22

BECAUSE JAMES ISN'T HIS BROTHER JESUS

I'm confused.

Which one is it: Are we to confess our sins to God or to each other?

First John 1:9 says: "If we confess our sins, he is faithful and righteous to forgive us our sins and to cleanse us from all unrighteousness." This verse, and the surrounding context, seems to imply that if a Christian confesses his or her sin *to God*, he or she will be forgiven.

Then James 5:16 says: "Therefore, confess your sins to one another and pray for one another." Here it seems like James is urging Christians to confess their sins to one another and not to God. James isn't prohibiting confessing sin to God; he is just emphasizing confessing to each other.

So, which one is it? Should Christians confess their sins to God, or to one another, or to both?

This is important. We want our prayers to be as worthwhile as possible. We want them to be as powerful as possible, so we don't want to get this wrong.

Have you ever noticed in the Gospels, when Jesus interacted with people, He indicated that He already knew what the other person was thinking and what was in their heart (John 2:25; 13:11; Matt. 9:4; 12:25)? The Gospel of John includes a scene where Jesus was at the temple in Jerusalem during Passover, a festival in the Jewish community to commemorate God's dramatic rescue of His people from slavery in Egypt. While at the temple, Jesus saw people selling oxen, sheep, and pigeons, basically turning the temple into a marketplace for profit. Jesus' response was to drive the money changers and the animals out of the temple. In the process, the Bible says Jesus knocked over the tables of the money changers.

Knocked over tables? Yes. "But I thought Jesus was so peaceful and calm."

The temple was a mess, and the Jews, shocked at what happened, asked Him, "What sign will you show us for doing these things?" (John 2:18). Translation: "What are you doing? And what makes you think you have the authority to do it?"

Jesus responded to them: "Destroy this temple, and I will raise it up in three days" (v. 19).

The Jews responded with, "This temple took forty-six years to build, and will you raise it up in three days?" (v. 20). The Jews were thinking about brick and mortar. Jesus was thinking about flesh and bone—the temple of His body.

Much later in his Gospel, John records that after Jesus rose from the dead, the disciples remembered Jesus' words from this exact moment in the temple and put it all together that it was about Him—Jesus was prophesying His own resurrection when He was talking to the Jewish people.

For John, this was an important moment because it caused the disciples to believe in Jesus more.

Shortly after Jesus knocked the tables over in the temple, the Bible says many in Jerusalem believed in Jesus' name as they saw the signs that He was performing. Then the Bible says: "Jesus, however, would not entrust himself to them, since he knew them all and because he did not need anyone to testify about man; *for he himself knew what was in man*" (vv. 24–25, emphasis mine).

What does it mean for God to know what is in man?

In order to understand this more, I want us to read from John Chrysostom, who was one of the early church's great preachers. This is how he understood what it means for God to know what is in a man or woman:

> He who possesses the heart and enters into the mind gave no heed to outward words. Clearly knowing their temporary passion, he did not have confidence in them as with perfected disciples, nor did he entrust all his doctrines to them as to those who had already been made steadfast believers. To know the things which are in the human hearts belongs only to God who fashions the heart (Ps. 33:15). For you alone, it says, established the heart (1 Kings 8:39). Therefore he had no need of witnesses in order to learn the thoughts of his own creatures.[3]

---

[3] *John: Interpreted by Early Christian and Medieval Commentators*, translated by Bryan A. Stewart and Michael A. Thomas (Grand Rapids, Eerdmans, 2018), 85.

This is one of the reasons, back in chapter 6, it was really important to recognize that when we pray to God, we have to understand that we are praying to someone who already knows everything.

That doesn't mean we don't need to pray. Nor does it mean that somehow prayer is less meaningful. It is just a theological truth about God that we have to be aware of as we approach God in prayer.

It is also why it isn't such a bad idea that we should listen more and speak less after we ask God for things, like wisdom. He knows what we need and the way He intends to respond to your prayer.

But back to our question: Are we supposed to confess our sin to God or to one another? I think the answer is that we are supposed to confess our sin to God.

But what do we do with James 5:16 and James' urging that we confess to one another?

I think that when James tells us to confess our sins to one another, it has more to do with God than it does with us. I think James learned something from his big brother.

What he learned is that only Jesus knows everything, including what is in the heart of a man or woman. Everything remains the same. The prayer of a righteous person is powerful because it works. The way you possess the prayer of faith is by confessing your sins to one another and praying for one another.

When you pray this way, the suffering are comforted, the sick are healed.

But James isn't Jesus. James isn't God. He has to have another way of figuring out the righteousness of the person who is praying, because unrighteous prayer won't be powerful. Thus, James tells us to confess our sins to one another.

Why? Because if you are willing to confess your sins to one another, James has a good idea that you've already confessed that sin to God. And if you've already confessed that sin to God, you've been forgiven. If you've been forgiven, you've been cleansed. Cleansed from what? Unrighteousness.

If you've been cleansed of unrighteousness, that means you are righteous. If you're righteous, "the prayer of a righteous person is very powerful in its effect" (James 5:16).

Thus, confession to one another becomes the visible manifestation that you have inwardly confessed your sins to God, that you are righteous, and that your prayers *work*.

Let me ask you a question: If God has forgiven you, what's so scary about confessing your sin to someone else? If God hasn't held it against you, by what strength does a mere human have to hold it against you?

> Confession to one another becomes the visible manifestation that you have inwardly confessed your sins to God.

On the other hand, James is also very suspicious when Christians do not want to confess their sin to one another—not because he is frustrated you won't expose your dirty laundry. No, he is frustrated because your lack of willingness likely signals that your prayers are weak.

Why?

Because likely, you haven't confessed your sin to God yet, and because of that, you don't want to confess them to anyone else either. In other words, a lack of confession to others signals that your prayers probably don't have the necessary power to do great things. Your lack of confession to others becomes the visible manifestation of a prideful heart that doesn't want to speak of its sinfulness to God.

That's why I think when James tells Christians to confess their sins to one another, it has way more to do with God than it does with us.

Next time you need someone to pray for you, perhaps you should avoid the person who seems like he or she never struggles. Not just because he or she is annoying, but maybe because he or she doesn't ever seem to talk about sin in his or her own life. I think James would be suspicious of this person. Maybe instead, you should find the person you know confesses his or her sin. Maybe even confesses that sin to other people. Because when you find that person, I think in that moment you've found powerful prayer.

One final thought for the moment: sometimes in order to find powerful prayer, you have to be the one who goes first.

PART V

KEEP PRAYING; GOD ISN'T ANNOYED

(A STUDY IN LUKE)

*We must repeat the same supplications not twice
or three times only, but as often as we have need,
a hundred and a thousand times. . . . We must
never be weary in waiting for God's help.*

—John Calvin

INTRODUCTION
TO PART V

As a result of the work of Christ, every Christian has a significant amount of freedom when it comes to prayer. One of the only requests from God is that we pray from a humble heart.

That is what part V is about. God's desire is that we pray for a lot of different things, but He also wants us to pray a lot for one particular thing.

Contrary to what feels permissible, when Christians pray out of humility, they have the freedom to be bothersome, annoying, and even impudent in prayer.

The goal here is to break cultural assumptions and norms about when and how to pray. Spiritually, it is through persistent prayer that the petitioner is shaped into just the right vessel fit to hold the answer when it comes.

CHAPTER 23

WHY DID YOU STOP?

I love my kids, but they can be annoying. Like, really annoying. When they get it in their five- and three-year-old heads that they want something, they won't stop asking until they get it.

"Daddy, can I have some Skittles?"

"Daddy, can I have just one Skittle?"

"Daddy, I promise I'll still eat dinner."

"Daddy, can I just have a little bite?"

"Daddy, what does 'suppress your appetite' mean?"

"Daddy, how about I have half of it now, and if I eat dinner, I can have the other half?"

"But Daddy, does that sound like a good plan?"

Sometimes I wonder if they really wanted the Skittles or if they have more fun negotiating.

As a parent, it wears you down and drives you crazy, because you can only say no so many times before you eventually just say, "Fine!"

I am the son of a salesman—an insurance salesman, to be exact. My dad has worked for the same company his entire career (almost forty years!). At one point, I asked my dad if I could go into the family business. He said, "No. You'd be awful."

Did I mention my dad is a straight shooter?

Then he said, "Son, you cannot take no for an answer when you get into sales."

Okay, he's right. I'd be awful. The second someone said, "No!" I'd say, "Sounds good. Thanks, and have a nice day!"

Recently, my dad watched firsthand Kaden working his magic on Lolly and me. As he observed in awe how Kaden eventually got what he was negotiating for—which I think was one more episode of *Curious George*—my dad said, "Wow, kids make the best salesmen. They never take no for an answer."

I had never heard my dad say that before, so I asked if that was a common expression in sales. He said, "No, I've just never noticed it before."

As weird as this might sound initially, Kaden and Oliver are examples of what prayer looks like.

Not all of prayer, but a significant part of it.

Earlier I described Kaden and Oliver as annoying, but there is another way to describe them. They are persistent. And being persistent in prayer is actually a good thing. Jesus even says so much about it in Luke's Gospel.

Kids are inherently persistent. They are naturally single-minded and unrelenting when they want something. God's desire is that His children would pray about lots of different things, but He also wants Christians to pray a lot for one thing.

The idea that a Christian would pray concerning a variety of things sounds like something you'd expect. Throughout the day a Christian might thank God for His provision. Perhaps request something from God. Maybe ask for wisdom or guidance about something important. Or there are those moments throughout the day when a Christian confesses his or her sin to God.

But if I had to guess, it isn't very natural for Christians to pray for something—one thing—over and over and over throughout the day, month, year. Why not?

Maybe we feel like prayer requires a certain decorum. That praying repetitively for something is bad etiquette and could diminish our chances of God answering our prayers. As a result, for the sake of being polite, we stop praying about this matter because God didn't answer us the first few times.

Maybe something in us feels bad, almost like we are annoying God. Perhaps we have been bothered in the past, for example, by really cute five- and three-year-olds named Kaden and Oliver. And because we have been bothered so much in the past, we know what it feels like to be annoyed, and because we know what it feels like to be annoyed, we can only imagine how irritated God must be all the time when His billions of children are repeatedly asking for things.

Thus, we conclude that God doesn't enjoy this.

However, just because we don't have the patience to be bothered, does that mean that God doesn't have the patience to be bothered too? What if it isn't fair to hold God to our standards of patience?

Maybe you have prayed a lot about this one really important circumstance in your life. Anyone who has had parents get a divorce can relate to this. You prayed and prayed and pled that your parents wouldn't get a divorce. Yet you never got an answer from God.

And because you never received an answer, you concluded that you were asking for the wrong thing, or perhaps what you asked for wasn't part of God's will. As a result, you just stopped praying about it. Maybe even worse, you stopped praying altogether.

> What if it isn't fair to hold God to our standards of patience?

It takes a lot of time and effort to pray persistently for something, to constantly think about it and share your thoughts with God about it.

But maybe there is something more to persistently praying than merely getting what you want from God. Maybe there is another reason Jesus tells us to pray like this—a nearness and comfort from God that we only experience while we are persistently praying about something.

I remember well the years leading up to my parents' divorce and those years following their separation. I was an adult, married, with kids, when my parents ended their marriage, and sometimes I wonder if it would have been easier if I was young and unaware of the situation.

Nevertheless, through my experience I've become convinced that when the Bible describes that two flesh become one in

marriage, this addition of 1 + 1 = 1 in marriage has so much
more meaning than merely having sex. Part of my reasoning has
to do with divorce. If in marriage two flesh become one, then
in divorce, one flesh has to become two flesh again. And as I
watched this, it is one of the most uncomfortable, dysfunctional,
and awkward things to observe.

During that long season I prayed a lot about my parents'
marriage, but over time I stopped praying. I'm sure there are a
lot of reasons why, but one was the comfortability I developed
within the situation.

I got used to it.

The more I got used to it, the less I prayed.

Once I realized nothing was going to change, I just settled
into an attitude of "it is what it is."

Perhaps you've settled into this attitude too and have gotten
pretty good at living in the mess—so much so, that prayer doesn't
seem necessary anymore. But is that a good enough reason to
stop praying? I hope not.

What about pride? Maybe pride prevents you from
persistently praying.

Pride? Yes, pride. But not just any kind of pride. This pride
masks itself as some kind of super spirituality.

I have a friend at church whose name is Steve. One Sunday
morning he pulled me aside and asked to pray. I said of course
and asked what it was that he wanted to pray for.

He told me that he was going through a really difficult
time, that his marriage had recently ended, he didn't have
the relationship he'd hoped to have with his kids, work was
inconsistent, and he was in bad shape. Yet, when you looked
at Steve, he appeared like everyone else. In other words, if he

didn't have the humility to tell me what was going on, I would have had no idea.

I put my hand on his shoulder and told him I was so sorry and asked again, "So, what can we pray for?"

Stop for just a moment.

I wasn't asking him a second time because I was rude or insensitive. I wasn't asking him again so that I could get him to relive the hell he was going through at that very moment. I asked him what we could pray for because, up to that point, all he had done was tell me what was going on; he didn't tell me specifically what to pray for.

He didn't say anything. Instead, he looked at me like, "I just told you what to pray for." I said, "Steve, you told me what is going on in your life, and there is a lot going on. Now we need to figure out what to pray for." He said, "Pray for my ex-wife, and pray for my kids."

I said, "Okay, let's pray for them." Then after we prayed for his ex-wife and kids, I said, "But what about you?"

He said, "Oh, I don't need prayer for myself. That's selfish, man. I don't ever pray for myself; I don't want to bother God with my problems."

In that moment, what Steve was trying to do was sound humble and self-sacrificial, because he was putting others before himself. He even put his ex-wife before himself. But really, he sounded spiritually lost and silly. His pride was so strong he didn't even see the need to ask God for help. He wanted to fix his problems on his own. In other words, he was saying to God, "I got this."

Given where his life was, I can't help but think that God's reaction was something like, "Do you, Steve?" (with a wry smile).

I suggested we could meet that week for coffee, and he agreed. It was a good conversation. I think it was needed for both of us. We talked a lot about prayer—specifically, persistent prayer and praying not only for others but himself too.

In many ways, life is still in the same place for Steve. What's different, though, is that he is persistently praying in the midst of it all now. I'm thankful for his friendship.

God's desire is for Christians to pray regularly about a lot of different things, but He also wants us to frequently pray for one thing too. It takes a great deal of humility to do that, to constantly go before God and ask for help over and over again.

There is a certain widow in the Gospel of Luke to whom Jesus is going to direct our attention in order to help us see this annoying and bothersome form of prayer.

CHAPTER 24

IMPUDENT PRAYER

Jesus told this story about a widow in Luke 18. And the whole point of this story was to convince His followers not to give up when they are praying.

When Christians continually pray, it actually reveals the kind of heart they have. And the kind of heart that is persistent in prayer is a heart that does not give up.

When you stop praying, you've given up. You've lost the heart of prayer.

The story goes like this:

> Now he told them a parable on the need for them to pray always and not give up. "There was a judge in a certain town who didn't fear God or respect people. And a widow in that town kept coming to him, saying, 'Give me justice against my adversary.'
>
> "For a while he was unwilling, but later he said to himself, 'Even though I don't fear God or respect people, yet because this widow keeps

pestering me, I will give her justice, so that she
doesn't wear me out by her persistent coming.'"

Then the Lord said, "Listen to what the
unjust judge says. Will not God grant justice to
his elect who cry out to him day and night? Will
he delay helping them? I tell you that he will
swiftly grant them justice. Nevertheless, when
the Son of Man comes, will he find faith on
earth?" (Luke 18:1–8)

The very first sentence of this parable demands our
attention. It says: "Now he told them a parable on the need for
them to pray always and not give up" (v. 1).

Right from the beginning we are told what this parable is
about. This wasn't one of Jesus' cryptic parables that He had to
explain later. We know from the get-go we are being called to
prayer. But not just any kind of prayer—the kind of prayer Jesus
had in mind is described as "always" praying. Continual prayer.
Perpetual prayer.

This is the same idea we find in 1 Thessalonians 5:16–
18, which says: "Rejoice always, *pray constantly*, give thanks
in everything; for this is God's will for you in Christ Jesus"
(emphasis mine).

We can also link this "always" kind of prayer back to an
earlier teaching in Luke's Gospel. In Luke 11 we find Jesus
praying, and when He finished, one of His disciples asked Him
to teach them how to pray.

Jesus answered:

"Whenever you pray, say,
Father,
your name be honored as holy.

Your kingdom come.
Give us each day our daily bread.
And forgive us our sins,
for we ourselves also forgive everyone
in debt to us.
And do not bring us into temptation."
(Luke 11:2–4)

This is a familiar prayer. Even a famous prayer. It's commonly referred to as the Lord's Prayer (see also Matt. 6:7–15).

But Jesus' teaching in Luke 11 concerning how to pray didn't end after He recited the Lord's Prayer. In other words, He wasn't done teaching His disciples how to pray. He went on to describe a particular scenario that is deeply personal.

Jesus asked them who of them had a friend that they could go to at midnight and ask for three loaves of bread because they've had some unexpected guests arrive and there is nothing for them to eat. And what if this friend just laid there in bed?

The Bible describes this person as still in bed, apparently listening to his friend calling out for food and thinking to himself: *Are you kidding me right now? Leave me alone. I was sleeping; the kids are still sleeping. Why are you bothering me?*

Jesus explained to the disciples that this friend wouldn't help and that his first inclination was to stay in bed, because that is what kind of heart this friend had. But at the end of the story, even this not-so-great friend got out of bed and gave his friend the three loaves of bread.

But why?

Jesus said, "Because of [this friend's] impudence he will rise and give him whatever he needs" (Luke 11:8 ESV).

Because of his impudence?

The Greek word for "impudence" is *anaideian*, and this is the only time it is used in the New Testament. This word can be understood as someone having or displaying poor etiquette.

This friend asking for bread at midnight showed impudence. He shamelessly ignored fundamental cultural norms in the Greco-Roman world related to hospitality. Simply, he was being rude. Yet he got what he wanted.

This man went to his friend's house way too late and disturbed the peace, but his need for food was greater than his concern for the time of day or whether anyone was sleeping. During this time period, you didn't do that. We wouldn't even do that today in our own culture. I sometimes won't answer if someone knocks on my door at noon, let alone midnight.

The friend knocking on the door so late showed a total lack of sensitivity. So much so, that the original audience hearing this would have totally understood if the friend never got out of bed.

But Jesus had other ideas. For Jesus, this is how you pray.

Jesus was trying to change the spiritual perception of prayer. What you once thought was a lack of sensitivity concerning how to pray, Jesus was now saying this is the *exact* way you should pray. Where you once thought it was careless to keep praying, Jesus is giving you the freedom to keep praying. Where you once were worried about your impudence, Jesus is giving you the freedom to be bothersome.

Remember, this whole scenario came about because one of the disciples asked Jesus to teach them how to pray.

Look at how Jesus responded after telling this story. Jesus said, "So I say to you, ask, and it will be given to you. Seek, and you will find. Knock, and the door will be opened to you. For everyone who asks receives, and the one who seeks finds, and to the one who knocks, the door will be opened" (Luke 11:9–10).

Let's go back to the beginning of Luke 11. Remember how Jesus set the scene? He said, "Suppose one of *you* has a friend and goes to him at midnight and says to him, 'Friend, lend me three loaves of bread, because a friend of mine on a journey has come to me, and I don't have anything to offer him'" (vv. 5–6).

Here is what I think Jesus was doing. He wanted the disciples to self-identify with the friend who went to the door, at the wrong hour, and woke everyone up. Woke up his children. Woke up the dogs. Woke up his neighbors.

Jesus did not want His disciples to pay attention to what is normal as it relates to prayer and talking to God; prayer is not normal, because the One to whom you are speaking is not normal.

He's God.

And human social norms don't apply when you talk to God. Any time is the right time to approach God in prayer. Even if it's the hundredth time.

Jesus wanted them to know they could go to His door and knock, and ask, and seek at all hours of the day. And when you feel like God is lying in bed, keep praying and don't lose heart. Don't give up, because God responds to impudent prayer.

> When you feel like God is lying in bed, keep praying and don't lose heart.

By the way, do you think it took a lot of humility for this friend to go to another friend's door at midnight and ask for help? Do you think he was a little embarrassed? Do you think he was nervous about waking up the kids?

Even though the Bible does not indicate it, the one knocking was there at the door due to his own insufficiencies. He needed help, and he knew where to find it.

Notice that the friend was *not* knocking on the door because he was powerful in the community and could demand what he wanted, when he wanted it. This friend did not show up at the door entitled to wake up this family to demand food. That's not how Jesus described this friend. He was humble, but he was also persistent, even at midnight.

Perpetual prayer is one element of humble prayer, according to Luke's Gospel. Let's turn our attention to another important element of prayer, according to Luke 18:1. That is, when we always pray, we should not lose heart.

Luke 18:1 (ESV) says: "And he told them [the disciples] a parable to the effect that they ought always to pray and *not lose heart*." The honest reality is that when we always pray, we make ourselves susceptible to discouragement.

I haven't hidden from you that it takes a lot of faith to pray—faith that God cares about your prayers even though it might feel like He doesn't; that He hears your prayers even though it feels like He hasn't; that He already knows what you need before you pray it; that He wants to answer your prayers even though He hasn't.

In this instance, most likely, the disciples might have lost heart because they had not received what they were praying for. But what was Jesus' desire? It was for them to not *egkakein*. This is an interesting Greek word. It can mean to not lose motivation, not lose enthusiasm, and not be discouraged.

Another way you could translate Luke 18:1 could be: "And he told them a parable to the effect that they ought always to pray and never give up, be discouraged, or lose enthusiasm."

When we are persistently praying for something, chances are what we are praying for (or about) is really important to us—but also out of our control. This leaves us in a vulnerable and humble position before God. Spiritually, when we find ourselves vulnerable and humble before God, the environment is perfect for prayer.

However, out of fear and impatience, we might try to manufacture something to trust in, but this never fully satisfies as when God responds to prayer. Notice I didn't say *answers* prayer.

People who persistently pray are fully aware that they are unable to do anything about their need on their own, and so they continually go before God to seek help. Nevertheless, persistence in prayer reveals a side of humility that can lead to doubt and a loss of motivation to pray. Because each time prayer is offered with no answer in return, it can diminish the desire of the one praying to offer that prayer again.

The Christian says things like, "What's the point? I keep praying and nothing happens. I guess it is what it is."

Jesus wanted to make sure that His disciples were aware of this. Prayer isn't easy, but don't give up. The remedy to this kind of discouragement is not to stop praying. It is not to generate something of our own to believe in or claim as answered prayer. According to Jesus, the remedy is to keep praying. Something supernatural happens when we keep praying—when we don't give up.

Each time we resist the temptation to give up, God builds within us the spiritual discipline of trust. Trust that God is sovereign. Trust that His providence is good. Trust that His ways are good—even if we can't sense that goodness in the exhausting moments of persistent prayer. This kind of trust in God is only developed through repetition, something we can't obtain if we give up.

Going back to the scene from Luke 11, it might be helpful to think of it this way: showing up to someone's house at midnight and asking for help is what not losing heart looks like. Staying at that person's door while he or she is still lying in bed is what not losing heart looks like. Not leaving until you receive what you've asked for is what not losing heart looks like.

Keep showing up, Jesus tells us. This is at the heart of prayer.

CHAPTER 25

PERSISTENT, ANNOYING, BOTHERSOME PRAYER

As we learned from the last chapter, the disciples were told at the beginning of the parable of the persistent widow what the point was. The point was that they were to always pray and never lose heart. In order to make this point, Jesus told them a story to help them visualize what it looks like to persistently pray and not give up.

Jesus said:

> "In a certain city there was a judge who neither feared God nor respected man. And there was a widow in that city who kept coming to him and saying, 'Give me justice against my adversary.' For a while he refused, but afterward he said to himself, 'Though I neither fear God nor respect man, yet because this widow keeps bothering me, I will give her justice, so that she will not beat me down by her continual coming.'"

> And the Lord said, "Hear what the unrigh-
> teous judge says. And will not God give justice
> to his elect, who cry to him day and night? Will
> he delay long over them? I tell you, he will give
> justice to them speedily. Nevertheless, when
> the Son of Man comes, will he find faith on
> earth?" (Luke 18:2–8 ESV)

This parable would have gotten their attention because it was expected that Jewish judges would defend widows when they were being taken advantage of. Take a look at these examples from the Old Testament:

> "You must not mistreat any widow or father-
> less child. If you do mistreat them, they will no
> doubt cry to me, and I will certainly hear their
> cry. My anger will burn, and I will kill you with
> the sword; then your wives will be widows and
> your children fatherless." (Exod. 22:22–24)

> Do not deny justice to a resident alien or father-
> less child, and do not take a widow's garment
> as security. Remember that you were a slave in
> Egypt, and the LORD your God redeemed you
> from there. Therefore I am commanding you to
> do this. (Deut. 24:17–18)

> God in his holy dwelling is a father of the
> fatherless and a champion of widows. (Ps. 68:5)

However, this judge was different. This judge didn't fear God, and because of that, he was numb to his obligations to look after this widow.

During this time period, widows personified weakness and vulnerability. Without a doubt, a widow was the most vulnerable adult in the culture. They were vulnerable sexually and were often poor. So what was the injustice that caused the widow to go to the judge? We don't know exactly. Jesus never told us that detail.

There is a chance that this widow desired to receive support from her deceased husband's financial settlement. But sadly, she kept coming up short.

It was common, in the case of death, for the wife to receive the agreed-up amount of money that would have been given to her in the case of divorce. According to custom, the wife was able to stay in her deceased husband's house and be supported by his estate until the settlement was paid.

Making matters more hurtful, the "adversary" was likely not a random person, but a member of the husband's family who refused to give her the marriage settlement.

But Jesus then described this widow as "bothering" the judge, because she continually went before him to demand justice. In the end, this bothering caused the judge to think to himself, "Though I neither fear God nor respect man, yet because this widow keeps bothering me, I will give her justice, so that she will not beat me down by her continual coming" (Luke 18:4–5 ESV). This woman's constant badgering caused the judge's eventual support against her adversary.

In the end, he didn't grant her justice because he loved God and respected humanity, or that he somewhere along the way became humble. No. According to Jesus, it was her persistence that made it happen. And this kind of persistence wasn't pretty.

She was so persistent that the judge felt as though he had been "beaten down" by her. This phrase is awesome. Talk about girl power. "Beat down" in Greek is *hupopiaze*, which literally means to blacken one's eye or to strike someone in the face. The verb translated "beat down" was a boxing term for when someone was hit below the eye.

The apostle Paul used this word to reference the beating his body had taken so that he was able to subdue his body and keep it under control (1 Cor. 9:24–27).

This judge was so worn out by this widow's continual pestering for justice that he felt like he'd been punched in the face.

It's almost like the judge ended up more afraid of this widow's browbeating than he was of God.

Jesus then explained that God is like a better version of this judge. If this unrighteous judge could give what the widow was asking for, how much more will a righteous God give justice to His elect? I believe that answer is a lot more.

When God's children cry to Him day and night, He will not delay long in answering their prayer (Luke 18:7–8).

Notice what did not happen when Jesus reflected on the story. The widow was not condemned for bothering this judge or beating him down or punching him in the face. Instead, she was rewarded for such persistence. She was upheld as a model for Christians in prayer. The only difference between her and us is that we are not persistently badgering an unrighteous judge; rather, we are praying to God, who is completely righteous.

> When God's children cry to Him day and night, He will not delay long in answering their prayer.

Let's return to Luke 18:1 for a moment, where we are called to always pray and never lose heart. After reading the parable we know a little more about what it means to always pray. For Jesus, Christians should always pray for a lot of different things, but it also becomes clear that Christians should persistently pray for just one thing.

This widow revealed that praying for one thing over and over and over again is okay. In her case, it was justice against her adversary.

You might be thinking at this point, *That's a bit scary to tell Christians to keep praying over and over again. What if what they are asking for isn't good or, worse, not part of God's will?*

The key to this kind of prayer is that the one who is continually praying is humble. It's humble, persistent prayer that Jesus upholds and welcomes.

This woman was alone, socially fragile, and at the mercy of a judge to protect her. She was not praying from a position of power—just the opposite, in fact.

When we are humble, we don't need to worry about persistently praying for the wrong thing. Why? Because when God reveals to humble people the kind of heart they have, humble people say, "I'm sorry; please forgive me."

Prideful people are a different story. When God reveals to these individuals the kind of heart they have, they reject God's revelation and keep praying for whatever they want.

These prayers won't get them very far. It's not because God doesn't hear them—He hears all prayer—it's just that prideful people are unable to hear God's response.

In our story, there was never a question about whether what the widow was praying for was the right thing. It's assumed it was. Why? I don't know, but I have a guess. Probably because she was humble.

Let's keep going. There is one more really interested thing that happens in Luke 18 that will help us better understand the importance of prayer and humility.

Right after Jesus explained the parable about the persistent widow and the unrighteous judge, He told another parable about prayer. But this time it involved a Pharisee and a tax collector.

In your Bible you likely have headings in bold that tell you about the different sections in the Bible. For example, above Luke 18:1–8 it probably reads something like, "The Parable of the Persistent Widow," and above Luke 18:9–14, probably something like, "The Pharisee and the Tax Collector."

While these two parables are different because they have different plots and characters, when you read them together, it's as though Luke has connected these two smaller stories to make one big story about prayer.

Luke 18:9 says: "He [Jesus] also told this parable to some who trusted in themselves that they were righteous and looked down on everyone else."

Luke is continuing the theme of righteousness—the judge from the previous parable was unrighteous, and now one of the key characters in this next parable was prideful and unrighteousness as well.

Prideful?

Yes.

Notice that it's a matter of the heart. Prideful people have the kind of heart that trusts in themselves.

Jesus then describes the Pharisee as "standing" to pray (Luke 18:11). Initially, the word for "standing" (*statheis*) might not seem that significant.

However, "standing" in Greek begs you to imagine someone making his or her way to the center of a stage. And while standing before everyone, this person is prepared to make a speech.

Matthew 6:5 alludes to this as well: "Whenever you pray, you must not be like the hypocrites, because they love to pray standing in the synagogues and on the street corners to be seen by people."

That's what "standing" here means. But the Pharisee wasn't going to make a speech. Jesus said he went to the temple to pray.

What the people saw and heard was a prayer. Maybe some of the people were even impressed by it. What Jesus saw and heard was the Pharisee's heart. And his heart revealed that his "prayer" was less about humbly talking to God and more like walking up to a podium to give a speech.

Nevertheless, the Pharisee prayed: "God, I thank you that I'm not like other people—greedy, unrighteous, adulterers, or even like this tax collector. I fast twice a week; I give a tenth of everything I get" (Luke 18:11–12).

When you trust in yourself for your righteousness, this is what your prayer sounds like.

The tax collector also prayed, but not in front of people—he couldn't imagine doing that.

Instead, he stood far off. The Bible says he wouldn't "even raise his eyes to heaven but kept striking his chest and saying, 'God, have mercy on me, a sinner!'" (v. 13).

In response to these two men, Jesus said, "I tell you, this one went down to his house justified rather than the other, because everyone who exalts himself will be humbled, but the one who humbles himself will be exalted" (v. 14).

I love that Jesus never told which man it was who went down to his house justified. It's obvious. And what makes it so obvious is the humility—or lack thereof.

With humility the tax collector offered his prayer of confession to God, and Jesus wanted the people to know that this was the justified man in their midst.

This would've been a shock to the audience because tax collectors were hated in their culture. *Tax collector* was a title that caused an emotional response similar to describing someone as a hypocrite, traitor, and sinner.

Yet according to Jesus, the tax collector was justified because he confessed his sin. And we know that when someone confesses his or her sin, he or she is brought back to the light and cleansed from all unrighteousness (1 John 1:9).

So how do we read Luke 18:1–8 and Luke 18:9–14 together? The glue that holds these two parables together is a combination of humility and prayer.

Follow me on this for a second.

In Luke 18:1–8 we read about a widow who persistently prayed for justice against her adversary. She was asking for something. Then in Luke 18:13–14 we read about a tax collector begging God for forgiveness because he was a sinner. He was asking for something.

Do you remember in chapter 16 when we talked about an inclusio? An inclusio is a literary device that uses the same word, phrase, or idea at the beginning and end of a section. Since the original Greek didn't have any verses and paragraphs, Luke had to be creative with how he was going to get the reader to pay attention to what was important.

Here, I think we have another inclusio formed around the idea of prayer and humility.

What is common to both the widow and tax collector? They are both stories about prayer. Jesus even told us to pray like them. Each story is about someone asking for help.

They aren't stories about merely getting things we want—like asking a genie in a bottle for a new house, or new job, or more clothes, or perhaps a nice vacation. The widow's and tax collector's prayers weren't about stuff. Both were asking from a position of humility and out of a humble heart.

But what happened in the middle of their prayers? Right in the middle was the Pharisee, and he was praying too. Well, it resembled more of a speech than a prayer. And what he was proclaiming was not his need for help, but instead, he told God about his own righteousness.

Luke 18:1–8 (Widow)	Praying and asking God for help is a good thing.
	Persistently praying for one thing is perfectly acceptable.
	Jesus answers the prayers of the humble.
Luke 18:9–12 (Pharisee)	Not asking God for anything demonstrates a lack of humility.
	Jesus even likens this to a speech, not prayer.
Luke 18:13–14 (Tax Collector)	Praying and asking God for help is a good thing.
	Begging God for one thing is a good thing.
	Jesus answers the prayers of the humble.

Let's not miss what Jesus did. He demonstrated through this story that when you pray like the Pharisee, it isn't really a prayer. As far as God is concerned, it's more like a self-exalting speech.

Yet Christians are admonished to pray like the widow or tax collector. We are encouraged to pray persistently, impudently, constantly, and passionately for help. And people who pray this way are humble, because they are fully aware of their needs and their own inability to meet those needs.

When you pray like the Pharisee, it isn't really a prayer.

CHAPTER 26

SOMEBODY CHANGES, BUT IT'S NOT GOD

Jeremiah 18 contains some beautiful imagery that I don't want us to miss. It's about clay and a potter. In Jeremiah 18, God gave a prophecy to a young man named Jeremiah—which wouldn't have been so strange, because earlier in the book we find out that Jeremiah was a prophet. And so, Jeremiah was just doing prophet stuff.

Jeremiah was a humble man, chosen by God to represent Himself to the people. Jeremiah was young and insecure. He came from a small town. He served a small community. And yet, God had big plans for Jeremiah.

Jeremiah wore his heart on his sleeve—he's often called the "weeping prophet"—because as God would expose Israel's heart, this prophet would weep and mourn.

Yet Jeremiah persevered and pursued the people of God so that they would repent of their sins and return to the Lord with their whole hearts. This has led some scholars to offer another moniker to describe Jeremiah: "the *persevering* prophet."

The way in which Jeremiah responded to God's call to be a prophet revealed the kind of humility within his heart. The Bible says that the Word of the Lord came to Jeremiah and said: "I chose you before I formed you in the womb; I set you apart before you were born. I appointed you a prophet to the nations" (Jer. 1:5).

In other words, there was nothing for Jeremiah to boast about or for him to take credit for. He was chosen by God to do this specific thing since before the world began.

Jeremiah's response to God was: "Oh no, Lord God! Look, I don't know how to speak since I am only a youth" (v. 6).

Jeremiah was so humble here. His response to God wasn't that he'd been waiting all his life for this moment. It wasn't that he was ready. It wasn't that he'd been training for this and had the right degree. It wasn't that he'd been on all the job boards and had the experience.

Nope.

Instead, his response was to say, "Lord, You should probably choose someone else. Someone older, wiser, more experienced," which was probably exactly why God chose him.

Then the Lord put out His hand and touched Jeremiah's mouth; apparently, this gave him all the powers he would need to do prophet stuff (v. 9).

Right away Jeremiah went for a test-drive.

Wouldn't you?

God said a few different times to look over there. "What do you see, Jeremiah?" And Jeremiah responded, "I see a branch of an almond tree" (v. 11).

Again, God asked Jeremiah: "What do you see?" And Jeremiah said, "I see a boiling pot, its lip tilted from the north to the south" (v. 13).

In each instance, God explained to Jeremiah what he was seeing. God showed Jeremiah that this wasn't rocket science. It was trust. Just tell the people what you see. Then God said it was time to get to work (v. 17).

Skip a few chapters to Jeremiah 18. Here, God told Jeremiah to get up and go down to the potter's house, because He wanted Jeremiah to hear His words. From there Jeremiah went to the potter's house and saw the potter at work at his wheel (Jer. 18:2–3).

Jeremiah noticed that the clay the potter was working on wasn't molding correctly in the potter's hand; it almost appeared to be spoiled. Yet being an experienced potter, he was able to rework the clay into another vessel. In the end, the potter was pleased with his creation (v. 4).

Then the Word of the Lord came to Jeremiah:

> "House of Israel, can I not treat you as this potter treats his clay?"—this is the LORD's declaration. "Just like clay in the potter's hand, so are you in my hand, house of Israel. At one moment I might announce concerning a nation or a kingdom that I will uproot, tear down, and destroy it. However, if that nation about which I have made the announcement turns from its evil, I will relent concerning the disaster I had planned to do to it." (vv. 6–8)

Notice He hadn't destroyed anything yet. God simply explained what would happen if the people didn't confess their sin and turn back to the Lord. In other words, God can rework the clay into something other than disaster.

Then the Lord said:

> "At another time I might announce concerning
> a nation or a kingdom that I will build and plant
> it. However, if it does what is evil in my sight
> by not listening to me, I will relent concerning
> the good I had said I would do to it." (vv. 9–10)

Again, God hadn't given any blessing yet. However, God explained that He was able to rework the clay into something other than good if the people did not listen to His voice.

In each example, God desired to do good; now it was up to the people to turn their hearts toward the Lord.

Now, what if we interpreted this passage prayerfully like we've done so many other times thus far?

The theme of part V revolves around the idea that Christians should not only pray for lots of different things, but also pray for one specific thing over and over again. This kind of prayer frightens many Christians. But what's so scary about being persistent in prayer?

Perhaps many are fearful of giving sinful humans the confidence to pray persistently for something. They are fearful that someone might repeatedly pray for the wrong thing. And worse, what if God ends up giving someone what they have erroneously prayed for over and over again, just like the widow and the judge (Luke 18)?

That might be a valid fear. And probably a lot of this fear is rooted in a good desire to uphold and honor God in the sacred moments of prayer.

But what are we really saying about God and His ability to handle prayer in those moments?

It seems as though this fear gives humans far too much credit. To use the imagery from Jeremiah 18, it's almost like there is a fear that the clay has the ability to tell the potter how to mold it or what kind of vessel it would like to be. But does Jeremiah give you the idea that the potter was ever afraid of the clay? Or that the potter was interested in what the clay would like to become?

What if, instead, through persistent prayer, it isn't God who wears down, but us?

Like clay in the gracious hands of the Potter, over time, we are worked and fashioned into just the right vessel the Potter has envisioned all along. It's the clay that has to endure and persist in the hands of the Potter.

Vessels are not crafted in one spin of the wheel. Not in merely two or three either, but in many repeated spins, all with the same intent. The potter's intent.

So are the prayers of Christians who persistently pray. What if, as we continually pray for something, persistently pray for something, something mysteriously begins to change in us? This change might very well be new to us, but not unknown to God.

In fact, this was part of the design process. In other words, if a Christian resists God in prayer due to his or her fear of persistently praying for something, he or she may never experience the essential change he or she was meant to undergo. That Christian will remain an unworkable lump of clay.

I want to return to when my parents were going through their divorce. I remember praying a lot that they wouldn't split up. A lot of people were praying that for them. Honestly, I think at times my parents were praying the same thing!

During this long season, as I was praying for this one specific thing over and over again, I often wondered why God was not doing something. Anything.

If a Christian resists God in prayer due to his or her fear of persistently praying for something, he or she may never experience the essential change he or she was meant to undergo.

God does hate divorce, right (Mal. 2:16 MSG)? And I'm praying for divorce not to happen, right? So why not step in to stop something you hate, God?

Yet I kept praying over and over again. Looking back, I wasn't accepting my role as clay. I wanted to be the Potter. I knew what was best. I had thought through this more than the Potter, and my plan, my desires, were best.

Then something changed in my heart.

It wasn't that now I wanted my parents to get a divorce. But my heart changed as I accepted that I was merely a lump of clay in the hands of God. In that moment, I finally felt comfort, security, and confidence.

My prayers began to change.

It's hard for me to describe, but it was as though I realized God was mourning with me. It was like I began to understand that God had been answering all my questions, but I was too loud to hear Him.

He was telling me, "Of course, I hate divorce. Yes, this is a good thing to pray for. Kyle, I'm mourning with you. Seek comfort in Me."

I did, and He comforted me. This experience in prayer was so important for me. His comfort was what I needed all along. It's what God was wanting me to ask for all along.

As I reflect on it, I keep coming back to this strange conclusion that I found the comfort I needed because I kept praying. Here is what's crazy: I found the comfort I needed because I kept praying for something else.

Like the clay, I needed to be shaped into just the right vessel to receive God's answer to my prayer. Molding me into this vessel was a long process, and God was so gracious to me throughout it all. Even gracious enough to endure my persistent prayers for something else.

I think God uses our persistent prayer to change us. It's not necessary for us to fear that God will change. Rest assured, He can't. He's God. Or that He will give you something that will ultimately bring harm because you have prayed for it over and over. He won't. He only gives good gifts (James 1:17).

> God uses our persistent prayer to change us.

Prayer is meant to change us. Persistence in prayer molds the petitioner into a vessel fit to hold the answer when it comes.

In other words, keep praying.

God is gracious as He shapes us. When we humbly pray over and over about something, we are right where we need to be.

We are in the process of being molded by the Potter into a very specific vessel which, in God's time, will be ready to receive His answer.

PART VI

UNANSWERED PRAYER

Every war, every famine or plague,
almost every death-bed,
is the monument to a petition
that was not granted.
—C. S. Lewis

INTRODUCTION
TO PART VI

The topic of unanswered prayer invokes a lot of different emotions. The spiritual reality is that we will all experience unanswered prayer at some point in our lives. Universally, it leaves the one praying asking: Why?

Generally, we are not too excited about the idea that God didn't answer our prayer. I guess there might be a few instances in which, looking back, we might be thankful that God didn't end up answering our prayer. (I mean, did you really want to be married to *that* guy?) Nevertheless, when we pray, there is a hope, an expectation, that God will not just hear, but answer our prayer.

In part VI, we will think through some of the possible reasons prayer is not always answered, and we'll even consider the possibility that maybe there isn't as much unanswered prayer as we think. Maybe we have even prematurely identified some prayers as unanswered.

My hope is that we might begin to see that unanswered prayer is more than merely coming to terms with the idea that

God doesn't care, or that God didn't hear you, or that He can't do what we are asking, or even that it wasn't part of God's will. Maybe, just maybe, there are other theological reasons for God not answering prayer.

CHAPTER 27

CONSIDER THE LILIES

U p to this point, with the help of a lot of different people—
like a widow, a tax collector, Jesus' younger brother, the
disciple Jesus loved, a few kings, some clay, a potter, and some
guy wanting bread late at night—we've concluded that it's okay
to pray for lots of different things. Not only that, it's okay to
persistently pray for one thing. Jesus even encourages us not to
worry about whether we're bothering God, that cultural norms
go out the window with prayer. Jesus simply wants us, with a
humble heart, to talk to God.

However, prayer of this kind could easily be twisted or
misunderstood. It might seem selfish or self-absorbed to pray for
things over and over again.

Yet notice what it is the individuals in these stories were
praying for. It wasn't power, money, a big new home, fancy cars,
or luxurious vacations. The widow desired justice against her
adversary. The tax collector begged for forgiveness. In James,
we're told to pray the prayer of faith. This is the kind of prayer
that heals people. The disciple Jesus loved desired Christians

to walk in the light by confessing their sins. King Jehoshaphat asked for protection against his adversary. King Solomon asked for wisdom to lead God's people. The clay submitted itself to the potter in order to become just the right vessel. And the friend wanted bread to feed his visitors.

These are all examples of humble people seeking help from God through prayer. They are humble people fully aware of their own insufficiencies and inabilities.

But what are we supposed to do when God doesn't answer our prayers? Who is to blame? Is it our fault? Does God not care? Is it simply not His will? Is God giving us the silent treatment in hopes that we will eventually figure out that He isn't going to answer our prayer?

What if there is a subtle difference between specifically praying for something over and over again and telling God how to answer your prayer over and over again?

What if determining the difference is only possible as you understand the kind of heart that is creating your prayers? The words you pray might sound like a simple request being made to God, while your heart tells a different story—one in which you're not only asking, but also *telling* God how to answer your prayer.

Let's think back to some earlier examples of prayer. Do you remember in Luke how the widow persistently bothered the judge to the point where the judge felt like he had been in a boxing ring and taken one too many hits below the eye? The Bible never says the widow told the judge *how* she wanted justice from her adversary. She didn't give a detailed account of how she wanted everything to unfold so that she could get her justice. The widow trusted that even this evil judge knew how to administer justice.

What about the tax collector? He didn't teach God about forgiveness and then, based on his theology and understanding of forgiveness, tell God how to forgive him. No, he was so humbled by his sin that he could barely muster up the words: "God, have mercy on me, a sinner!" (Luke 18:13). The tax collector trusted that God knew how to forgive him.

And James urges us to confess our sin to one another so that we might pray the prayer of faith. James tells us how to possess the prayer of faith; it then becomes a question as to whether we are willing to confess our sin and be healed. Nowhere does James indicate that obtaining the prayer of faith is up for redesign.

King Jehoshaphat was no different. In front of all the people he was leading, he asked God for protection. What he didn't do was tell God how to protect them. He knew better than that. He simply asked for protection and let God take care of the rest.

This isn't easy, though—especially if you have any vested interest in what you are praying for. It's really hard merely to pray and ask for help and then sit back and let God do the rest. Not because you don't think God is capable of answering your prayer; rather, you probably care a great deal about whatever is being prayed for. It might deeply impact your life and the lives of those you love. It makes sense that you have an idea of how best to resolve the issue.

It takes a lot of humility to pray and ask for help. But it also takes faith and humility to sit, listen, and observe how God is going to answer your prayer once it has been uttered.

I'm beginning to wonder if there isn't as much unanswered prayer as we might think. What if God has answered your prayer but you've missed it because you have been so persistent and stubborn in thinking that it will be answered in one particular way?

What if for the longest time you've thought God has not answered your prayer, when, in reality, He has?

What if the silence you have perceived from God was, in fact, stillness? Not because God won't answer your prayer, but because His work in answering your prayer is finished.

In other words, His work is done.

> What if for the longest time you've thought God has not answered your prayer, when, in reality, He has?

And because you've been expecting the answer just like you've always envisioned it, you missed God's answer.

God's response to prayer is found in His revelation to us. And the way He reveals Himself to us is vast, because His creation is huge and immeasurable.

This means that God has at His fingertips all of His creation to point to in order to respond to your prayer. For a good review, you might go back and reread chapter 5. (I'll wait for you right here.)

Using words like *vast* and *immeasurable* make it sound like it is going to be really hard to know when God has actually answered your prayer. It's like finding Nemo in the ocean.

Good luck.

In some ways, yes, it will be difficult. Not because God makes it so hard but rather, because sinful humans will figure out how to get in the way. God's revelation is clear, but because of our sin, we can't always see it clearly.

However, if you are humble and dependent upon God's revelation, He is gracious to help in times of need in order to reveal to you His answer and ultimately what you're looking for.

What are some of those ways in which God has revealed His answer indirectly through creation?

In the Sermon on the Mount, Jesus responded to the crowds that followed Him, that if they wanted to know about the kingdom of God, they needed to consider the lilies in the field and the birds in the air (Matt. 6:28).

When the people were desperate to know more concerning the kingdom of heaven, Jesus told them about a farmer sowing seeds.

When the disciples asked why He was talking to the people like this, Jesus responded: "Because the secrets of the kingdom of heaven have been given for you to know, but it has not been given to them" (Matt. 13:11). In other words, it had not been revealed.

According to Jesus, the disciples knew the secrets of the kingdom of heaven, and that wasn't because the disciples were better than everyone else. No, it was because Jesus had revealed it to them. As a result, Jesus taught the people that the kingdom of heaven was right under their noses—it could be seen in the soil they stood on, the lilies they walked by, the seeds they planted, and even in the farmers planting the seeds.

But the people were looking for different answers to their question. And because they had something else in mind, they missed it.

In Proverbs 30:24–28, we learn that if you want to become exceedingly wise, you don't merely read your Bible; you are to consider the ants, hyraxes, locusts, and lizards. Contemplating these creatures will lead you to know more about their Creator.

What about when the disciples asked Jesus to teach them how to pray? He recited what we've come to know as the Lord's Prayer. But Jesus also taught them about prayer using people and bread and social norms of the day (Luke 11:5–13).

Or how about when Jesus taught His disciples how they ought to pray, and He pointed to the culturally despicable tax collector and said to pray like him (Luke 18:9–14)?

When Jesus was asked how to pray, He didn't answer directly. He didn't just say, "Recite these words or sit in this posture or do these things." It was almost like He was preparing His disciples to hear from the Lord by observing the world around them.

Why?

Because Jesus knew that He would not always be with them. He knew that He was going to a place they couldn't go just yet. So if they were going to hear from the Lord, they were going to need to hear differently. They were going to need to see the world differently.

Maybe instead of thinking of God's answer to our prayer, through His revelation, as too vast and immeasurable and surely too difficult to adjudicate, we can think of His revelation as so expansive that it's almost impossible for us to miss— as long as we are humble and trust that God will make Himself known to us.

At the very end of the Gospel of John is a moment after Jesus rose from the dead, when the resurrected Lord revealed Himself to the disciples. John prefaces it by saying: "He [Jesus] revealed himself in this way" (John 21:1b). This is what God does—He reveals Himself.

John describes how Peter and many of the disciples (including John) were on a boat fishing, but they didn't catch anything all night (v. 3). As the sun was rising on a new day, Jesus was on the shore, and He asked the disciples if they had caught anything. Not realizing they were speaking to Jesus, they responded to this man that they hadn't. Then the man said, "Cast the net on the right side of the boat, . . .and you'll find some" (v. 6).

They listened and cast their nets in the area the man spoke of, and the load of fish they caught was so great and so heavy they were not able to haul it in.

Then Peter shouted from the boat, "It is the Lord!" (v. 7).

See, Jesus "revealed himself in this way" (v. 1b).

When was the last time you said that? A moment when you yelled, "It is the Lord!"

There is a certain kind of beauty when prayer makes the sacred transition from unanswered to answered. It is one of those opportunities for us to proclaim, "It is the Lord!"

But did you notice something? The prayer was already answered. Jesus was always Jesus. It wasn't that Jesus became the Lord when Peter proclaimed it; it was simply that the disciples became aware that the man beside the shore wasn't just a man. It was Jesus.

That's often how unanswered prayer works. God's answer is finished. He's revealed Himself.

It is just a matter of when you're able to see that the answer was, in fact, the man on the shore.

The wait is worth it. Finding God is always worth it.

Back to my earlier question: What if there wasn't as much unanswered prayer as we once thought? What if you could actually move some unanswered prayer to answered prayer? What if, in order to accomplish this, all you needed to do is move out of the way so that you can begin to see and hear how the Lord has revealed Himself as an answer to your prayer?

In order to do this, all that is required is humility. A humble heart patiently observes its surroundings to see if God has, in fact, answered the prayer.

> A humble heart patiently observes its surroundings to see if God has, in fact, answered the prayer.

This might mean that we get it wrong at times, where we think God has answered our prayer and He hasn't. That's okay. As we will discuss in the next chapter, God takes His time in revealing His answer to our prayer.

Humble hearts develop a habit of listening and observing after a prayer is offered. This kind of heart isn't anxious about how God is going to answer a prayer because it is aware of the limitless ways God can do that.

An anxious heart does just the opposite. This kind of heart is worried not only about whether God will answer a prayer, but the way in which God will answer it.

Have you ever had a pretty good idea that something was up? That someone might throw a surprise party for you? That someone had a surprise gift to give you? I don't like that feeling at all. Parties in general aren't my thing, let alone a surprise party!

Not too long ago, Lolly put together a surprise dinner with some of our closest friends and family to celebrate receiving my PhD from Dallas Theological Seminary. It was such a good night.

Lolly kept bugging me that we needed do something big to celebrate, and I kept saying, "Nah, it's not a big deal. Let's just go to dinner or something."

But I knew something was up.

When you suspect something is brewing, every place you go, you wonder, *Is this it?* Are you going to walk into the next room and find it full of people you love? And then you come to find out it's just another room. In a strange way, it can be an emotional letdown. It can be exhausting, because you are always prepared for what might be behind every door. But then the moment arrives, and you walk into the restaurant and find it filled with your closest friends and family.

Surprise!

In some ways you knew it was coming, yet in other ways, you had no idea how it was to unfold.

Humble hearts don't plan their surprise parties. Humble hearts trust that God's answer will always be better, so there isn't this need to force your will upon God's will. (As though that's even a possibility!)

> Humble hearts don't plan their surprise parties. Humble hearts trust that God's answer will always be better.

Prideful hearts are never quite able to make the transition from unanswered prayer to answered prayer, largely because they are convinced that their prayer should be answered in a particular way. The way they've envisioned it all along.

Don't miss this.

What is still so gracious about God is that He doesn't refuse to answer the prayers from a prideful heart.

No.

He answers even those prayers—but the one praying never gets the pleasure of experiencing "It is the Lord!" because he or she is stuck looking for his or her own answer.

And when you are stuck on your answer, prayers seem to remain unanswered.

CHAPTER 28

GOD DOESN'T HURRY

Have you been praying for something for a long time? So long that you are about to declare "unanswered prayer" and move on?

Hold on! Wait! Don't give up just yet.

One of the distinct characteristics God draws out of us when we pray is patience. He causes us to slow down and wait for His timing.

I think too many prayers, still in progress, have been prematurely declared "unanswered."

Why?

Probably because the one praying assumed it would be answered by now.

It takes too much patience and humility to sit and wait and watch for God's revelatory response to our prayer. In our world, it is far more natural to schedule a meeting or make a phone call when we need information. Our lives are designed so that we don't have to wait for much. We ask Siri or Alexa. We search Google. What we don't do is wait—especially for information.

I don't know about you, but I'm not a good waiter.

Lolly would say I'm a little impatient. Okay, okay, *really* impatient.

If you and I were to get together, I would likely show up ten minutes early. For whatever reason, I have this fear that I'm going to get a flat tire or run into traffic on my way. Then I'd just sit in my car or grab a table and take care of some emails and texts before our meeting began.

That sounded way too professional. Let's be honest: I'd check Facebook and Instagram.

Waiting for you to arrive wouldn't bother me at all. I'm mentally prepared for that. I actually had a hand in designing it to be that way.

But what does annoy me is when you're late.

Let's just say that when Lolly shows up, she is always right on time.

I can still remember being sixteen and driving over to Lolly's parents' house to pick her up. Remember, I'm always ten minutes early. I would sit in her living room, hanging out with her parents, while she finished getting ready for us to go out.

Her mom would always say, "What is taking that girl so long?" Who knew twenty years later how profound that question was? She's my favorite person to wait for. I'll wait for her any day. I might throw a little fit, though.

Recently, Lolly had this brilliant idea to set all our clocks in the house forward ten minutes so she could mentally get ready earlier. It actually worked!

What also happened is that I started showing up to places twenty minutes early!

Prayer has this unique ability, likely by design, to cause us to slow down and wait. I think one of the things God loves about those who are waiting for an answer is the conversations that take place. God delights when two followers of Christ talk through the possibility of God's revelation as an answer to prayer.

> "Do you think that was God's response to my prayer?"
>
> "Do you think He answered it?"
>
> "Wouldn't it be crazy if God answered your prayer that way?"
>
> "Who would have thought God would do that?!"

Those are deep conversations that require a spiritual awareness developed through the arduous practice of waiting. Those types of conversations could also be some of the initial interactions a person might have as he or she becomes more and more aware of spiritual things.

But it does require humility. Humble prayer embraces the fact that God doesn't hurry or rush, but acts in His perfect timing.

Sometimes we declare prayer unanswered because we are impatient, because God hasn't bound Himself by our time frame. But God is never early and never late. Just like Lolly, He is always right on time.

In 2 Peter 3:9 we learn about God's heart toward us. It says: "The Lord does not delay

> Humble prayer embraces the fact that God doesn't hurry or rush, but acts in His perfect timing.

his promise, as some understand delay, but is patient with you, not wanting any to perish but all to come to repentance."

Peter is describing God's character as patient.

The Greek word for "patient" is *makrothumei*, and it means that someone has demonstrated endurance or long-suffering despite difficulties. It can also mean that someone endures without complaint. That he or she has not lost heart—which is quite beautiful, since Peter is talking about salvation in 2 Peter 3:9.

God desires for all to come to believe in the Lord Jesus and be saved. God does not wish for any to perish without a belief in the Lord and, as a result, He remains patient toward us. God doesn't grow weary, doesn't get angry or annoyed, as He waits.

This promise in 2 Peter 3:9 is about salvation. But what about prayer? Does God reveal His patient heart toward us in prayer?

Yes, He does. Follow me on this.

I want to go back to an earlier passage we talked about. In Luke 18:1–8 Jesus told a story because He wanted to teach the disciples how to pray. And particularly the kind of heart they are to have when they pray. Jesus' desire was that they always pray and never lose heart.

Then He told a story about a widow, who bothered and bugged and wore down a corrupt judge in order to give her justice against her adversary. The judge ended up giving the widow her justice, but not because of the goodness of his heart. He just wanted her to go away.

Then Jesus responded to the disciples and basically said, "If this judge can give her justice, how much more will God give justice to those in need? How much more will God answer the requests of those who petition Him?"

The logical conclusion is that God will give them a lot more. Then Jesus said: "Will not God give justice to his elect who cry out to him day and night? Will he delay helping them?" (Luke 18:7).

Jesus used the same word from 2 Peter 3:9 to describe his patience toward you.

The verse reads, "Will not God grant justice to his elect who cry out to him day and night? Will he delay (*makrothumei*) helping them?" (Luke 18:7).

The patience that God has toward your prayers is the same kind of patience He has toward those who have not yet believed in the Lord for salvation.

By the way, is everyone going to be saved? Will everyone believe in the Lord Jesus?

Sadly, no.

Similarly, will every prayer that is offered be answered? No. But we know the heart of God.

It's patient. And until the time has passed and the prayer is unanswerable, might I suggest to keep praying?

One of my favorite moments in the classroom happens at the beginning of each class. I take out my iPad and Apple Pencil, and I ask if there is anything we can pray for or about.

It always takes the students a little time to get used to this moment, but by the third or fourth class, people are sharing all kinds of things for us to pray for.

In addition to praying for new things, we always return to previous requests that I've written down and see if anything has changed.

Sometimes we are able to thank the Lord for answered prayer, and other times we just keep praying, maybe even all semester, for this one thing.

I remember this one couple, Mary and Nicolas, from a course I was teaching at the seminary. It was about halfway through the semester when Mary spoke up. Well, she first looked at Nicolas, not to seek approval, but needing support from her husband. Nicolas graciously nodded his head as if to say, "I'm right here."

Mary, with tears in her eyes, began to tell the painful story that they were having a hard time getting pregnant, and to make matters worse, when they had gotten pregnant in the past, they had a hard time keeping the baby. They had experienced a few miscarriages and were really hurt and confused.

This had been going on for eighteen years.

They had tried everything, and Mary and Nicolas wanted to be parents so badly. Yet through it all, they loved the Lord. They trusted the Lord and His timing, even though it made no sense.

After Mary and Nicolas told us their story, I asked if it was okay if we prayed for them. They said yes. Then I asked if it was okay if we put our hands on their shoulders. They said of course. Then as a class, we surrounded Mary and Nicolas and prayed.

About a month later, near the end of the semester, I asked if there was anything we could pray for.

This time, Mary's hand shot up, and Nicolas looked at her, shocked, as if to say, "What are you doing?"

Mary then teared up again and said with her beautiful Kenyan accent, "I'm pregnant. And we're very scared."

She had just found out.

That is why Nicolas was so shocked.

Mary then told the class that she hadn't even told her family yet. She wanted us to be the first to know. Her prayer request now was for the delivery of the baby and that the baby would grow big and strong in her belly.

So we prayed.

The class ended, time moved on, but the prayers continued as I tried to keep in touch with Mary and Nicolas.

Then one day I was in Costco, in the way back where all the water bottles are. I saw this woman struggling to lift a case of water into her cart. I bent over and asked the woman if she'd like some help.

She stood up with her hand on her back and said, "Yes, thank you." It was Mary! She then said, "Ohhh, Doctor, Doctor!" And she gave me a giant hug. I'm not sure, but I think my feet left the ground. She told me all about their beautiful daughter named Sifa, which is a Swahili word for "praise." Mary and Nicholas wanted to praise God for giving them a child after waiting for eighteen years.

Just like God is patient toward us, we should be patient in return as we humbly wait for His timing.

This might look like holding off on declaring prayer unanswered; it might look like not losing heart that prayer is unanswered. Waiting for prayer to be answered is not easy. It can even be painful, depending on the circumstance. But remember, "The Lord does not delay his promise, as some understand delay, but is patient with you" (2 Pet. 3:9a), even in the midst of what feels like an unanswered prayer.

Let's keep going with this. I dare you not to laugh toward the end of this next story, and I promise you'll never think about a game of charades the same way ever again.

In the Gospel of Luke, we read about how in the days of King Herod, there was a priest named Zechariah. He was married to a woman named Elizabeth. The Bible describes them as a couple that loved the Lord and those around them (Luke 1:6).

It also describes them as having no children, not by choice, but because "Elizabeth could not conceive" (v. 7). In other words, the couple struggled with infertility.

Why does Luke go to great lengths to describe the holiness and righteousness of both Zechariah and Elizabeth? What if Luke does this in order to demonstrate that God is not a god of karma, that the reason Elizabeth struggled with infertility wasn't because God wanted to get her or Zechariah back for some past sin they committed?

What if, instead, Elizabeth struggled, like many, with the effect of the Fall upon her body with a physical abnormality that made it very difficult for her to have a child? Or maybe it was Zechariah whose body was incapable of producing offspring.

The Bible also says they were advanced in years, seemingly indicating that now Elizabeth was past the age at which she could conceive a child.

After introducing us to Zechariah and Elizabeth, Luke describes how Zechariah was chosen by God to go into the temple of the Lord and burn incense, according to the custom of the priesthood (v. 9). While in the temple of the Lord, the angel Gabriel appeared to Zechariah and scared the daylights out of him—which, in my opinion, is totally understandable.

He was looking at an angel. Like, a real one.

Gabriel's response to Zechariah was: "Do not be afraid, Zechariah, because your prayer has been heard. Your wife Elizabeth will bear you a son, and you will name him John.

There will be joy and delight for you, and many will rejoice at his birth" (vv. 13–14).

What has been answered?

According to Gabriel, he was sent by God to let Zechariah know that their prayer was finally going to be answered. A prayer that he and Elizabeth had probably been praying for years, maybe even decades. Maybe they had even declared that this prayer was not going to be answered, and God was now letting them know that He was ready to answer their prayer.

Zechariah's response to the angel is great. He says, "How can I know this? . . . For I am an old man, and my wife is well along in years" (v. 18). If you ever meet Gabriel, apparently, this isn't the correct response to his good news. Gabriel answered, "I am Gabriel, who stands in the presence of God, and I was sent to speak to you and to tell you this good news" (vv. 18–19). Then Gabriel hit the mute button on Zechariah, making him unable to speak until all that God had promised in response to Zechariah and Elizabeth's prayer took place.

In other words, God was going to answer their prayer even though Zechariah wasn't so sure how this would all work out.

Imagine this: Zechariah, mute, walked out of the temple, and the people were confused. They realized that he had seen a vision in the temple, but they couldn't communicate with him. Luke even says that Zechariah kept making signs to them so that they could understand.

Then the Bible says: "After these days his wife Elizabeth conceived and kept herself in seclusion for five months. She said, 'The Lord has done this for me. He has looked with favor in these days to take away my disgrace among the people'" (vv. 24–25).

I feel like what transpired has to be one of the greatest games of charades ever recorded.

Zechariah, unable to speak, had to go home and make signs to his wife, trying to communicate:

1. I had a crazy day at work, honey.
2. I met the angel Gabriel. He scared me.
3. He told me that we are going to have a baby.
4. I didn't believe Gabriel, so he caused me to be mute.
5. We need to have sex.

This is epic.

God answered their prayer; it just took a long time. For most of their lives they wrestled with this unanswered prayer, but from God's perspective it wasn't unanswered at all. What Zechariah and Elizabeth counted as slowness wasn't slow at all to God. In the end, their prayer was answered, and what was once unanswered prayer became answered prayer.

While we are on this topic of babies and prayer, there is another interesting story in the Bible. No charades are involved in this story, but there is certainly some questionable behavior, to say the least.

We find this story in Genesis 15. God promised Abraham that He was going to make a great nation from his lineage—a people so numerous that if you counted all the stars in heaven, you'd still not add up all of his descendants (v. 5). But Abraham's response to God was: "Lord GOD, what can you give me, since I am childless and the heir of my house is Eliezer of Damascus?" (v. 2).

God responded that Eliezer would not be Abraham's heir, that he would have his very own son. Then the Bible says that Abraham believed the Lord, and it was "credited . . . to him as righteousness" (v. 6).

Abraham and Sarah's prayer was for a child, who would be the heir of this great nation that the Lord had promised to give them. God's response was that He was going to answer their prayer. He promised they would have their very own son.

After some time had passed, Sarah and Abraham were growing more and more weary because they weren't getting any younger (Gen. 16:1). The Bible says they waited ten years for God to provide an heir (Gen. 16:3). I wonder how many times during those ten years they discussed whether this prayer might go unanswered.

Then they had an idea—maybe God's answer to their prayer all along was right in their midst?

Sarah's idea was that Abraham should sleep with Hagar, who was Sarah's servant (v. 2), and this child would be the heir God promised.

And you thought the Old Testament was boring and uneventful.

Well, Abraham listened to Sarah and slept with Hagar, and she conceived a child.

As you can imagine, this didn't end well. It was messy. Sarah's heart was broken. She treated Hagar with contempt and got really mad at Abraham.

Hagar, who was pregnant, was treated so poorly that she ran away. While at a spring of water in the wilderness, the angel of the Lord found her. Then the angel did something interesting: he blessed Hagar. And the blessing that the angel bestowed on

Hagar was similar to God's promised blessing to Abraham. The angel said that her offspring would be incalculable (v. 10).

The angel said that she was to name her son Ishmael. Hagar did what the angel said and named her son Ishmael. When she gave birth to Ishmael, Abraham was eighty-six years old (v. 11, 16).

This was intense. Well over a decade had passed since God's original promise that Abraham and Sarah would have their own son as an heir. In the meantime, Sarah and Abraham tried to take God's promise into their own hands. How'd that work out for them?

When Abraham was almost one hundred years old, God finally told him that the time had come when Sarah would conceive a child who would be his heir (Gen. 17:16).

What was Abraham's response? The Bible says he literally fell on his face and laughed as he thought to himself, "Can a child be born to a hundred-year-old man? Can Sarah, a ninety-year-old woman, give birth?" (v. 17).

God responded: "Your wife Sarah will bear you a son, and you will name him Isaac. I will confirm my covenant with him as a permanent covenant for his future offspring. As for Ishmael, I have heard you. I will certainly bless him; I will make him fruitful and will multiply him greatly" (vv. 19–20).

Please don't miss the grace of God. Abraham and Sarah had taken God's timing into their own hands and created a huge mess. Hagar had a love child with Abraham, and now Hagar was a single mom and alone.

Yet God, in the midst of the mess, still extended grace to Hagar and Ishmael by blessing them and promising to make them a great nation.

God also dealt graciously with Sarah and Abraham as He was about to give them their heir that they had been asking for all this time. The God of the Old Testament is not a mean God.

Finally, the Lord appeared to Abraham again and told Abraham that He was going to return the next year, and when He did, Sarah would have a son. What's great about this part of the story is that Sarah was in the tent listening to this conversation between the Lord and her husband. And just like her husband, Sarah started to laugh as she thought to herself, "After I am worn out and my lord is old, will I have delight?" (Gen. 18:12).

Translation: "Wait a second, this old lady is going to have sex and get pregnant?"

Watch God's response. He said, "Why did Sarah laugh, saying, 'Can I really have a baby when I'm old?'" (v. 13). God was like: "Is she laughing at me right now?"

Abraham and Sarah must have had a good sense of humor. Maybe, when you've been praying for something for so long, humor isn't a bad thing.

If that wasn't funny enough, then Sarah denied laughing at God (v. 15a). And God said, "No, you did laugh" (v. 15b)! God asks a really important question: "Is anything impossible for the LORD? At the appointed time I will come back to you, and in about a year she will have a son" (v. 14).

Nothing is impossible for the Lord—not even the prayer request you've been praying about for such a long time.

> Nothing is impossible for the Lord.

We have to resist the urge to give up on prayer so that we don't lose heart and rush too soon to the conclusion that this prayer has gone unanswered because God hasn't responded yet. We also have to resist the urge to generate something of our own to call answered prayer.

It takes humility to wait for God's timing. Yet God told Sarah and Abraham, "At the appointed time," (Gen. 18:14), which means in God's time.

You might be one hundred years old when it's God's appointed time. You might even laugh when it's God's appointed time. But keep praying, because you never know when it's His appointed time.

God is the only One who gets to declare prayer unanswered.

CHAPTER 29

PRAY, EVEN IF IT'S FOR THE WRONG THING

It's not all that uncommon to hear something like this about unanswered prayer: "Sometimes God doesn't answer prayer because you are asking for the wrong thing." There is some truth to this statement. But before we quickly settle into that conclusion, I want to wrestle with this idea.

Should a Christian stop praying for something because he or she thinks it might be wrong, or because someone else told him or her that it was wrong?

What if I do pray for something wrong? Is that sinful? Is God going to punish me? Should I apologize to God for praying about that and promise to never do it again?

Initially, one might assume that the correct answer would be yes. Typically, when we do something wrong, it's another way of saying it was sinful.

But I'm not so sure that's the case in prayer.

In some ways, that goes against everything I'm trying to do in this book.

To say that God won't answer your prayer because you are praying for the wrong thing gives way too much credit to the words you are praying. God is infinitely more interested in the heart that is producing your prayer than the words themselves.

Even wrong words.

God is big enough, smart enough, wise enough, and gracious enough to be able to handle when wrong things are prayed to Him.

> God is infinitely more interested in the heart that is producing your prayer than the words themselves.

In fact, the reality is that, due to ignorance or spiritual immaturity, I can pray for something wrong while at the same time have a good heart. Given the reality of sin and brokenness, it's likely that I pray a lot for the wrong thing. But I want you to pray more, not less. And I'm suspicious that the fear of praying for the wrong thing is causing you to pray less. It's as though you think you can't go wrong if you just don't pray.

As a result, you avoid talking to God.

But what if God is able to simultaneously hear your wrong question as you verbalize it and yet hear your heart behind the wrong question? Moreover, what if God chooses to respond to your heart?

The Bible is riddled with stories of Jesus interacting with His disciples, who asked the wrong questions. For example, there was this one time the disciples came to Jesus, full of pride, and asked: "Who is the greatest in the kingdom of heaven?" (Matt. 18:1).

They wanted to know which of them was going to be able to rule over the other disciples.

But this was the wrong question. Jesus responded to this wrong question by putting a child in the middle of them. He said that they must become humble, like this child, if they wanted to be great in the kingdom of heaven.

Another time, the mother of James and John (the sons of Zebedee) went to Jesus and asked if her two sons could sit next to Him, one at the right and the other on the left, in the kingdom of heaven (Matt. 20:20–21).

Can you imagine? *Mom! What are you doing?!* This is like when your mom licked her finger to wipe food off your cheek in front of all your friends.

Oh, your mom didn't do that? Totally, me neither. Whose mom would ever do that?

Even though this is the wrong question, Jesus graciously responds with the heavenly logic that if you'd like to be first in the kingdom of God, you must be a servant. Those great in God's kingdom are those who serve one another. Jesus even used Himself as an example: "Just as the Son of Man did not come to be served, but to serve, and to give his life as a ransom for many" (Matt. 20:28).

And what about doubting Thomas? Remember when he told the disciples after he heard the reports that Jesus had risen from the dead that unless he saw Jesus' hands and the marks from the nails, and until he touched Jesus' side, he wouldn't believe? Eight days later, Thomas was with the disciples and the doors were locked, yet Jesus entered the room.

This visit by Jesus seemed to have a specific purpose, because Jesus said to Thomas, "Put your finger here and look at my hands. Reach out your hand and put it into my side" (John 20:27a).

The Gospel of John doesn't indicate that Thomas ever prayed or asked God for this opportunity. It simply says he told the disciples that he wouldn't believe unless . . .

But even though Thomas never asked specifically, Jesus heard the question of his heart and answered it.

Even though it was the wrong question.

Then Jesus answered the more significant question from Thomas' heart. He told him, "Blessed are those who have not seen and yet believe" (John 20:29b).

Even though Thomas sought the wrong thing, Jesus still graciously gave Thomas the answer he was hoping for. By acting graciously toward Thomas, Jesus didn't validate his wrong question. He looked past the wrong question and provided the real answer: *blessed are those who believe but do not see*. Jesus receives wrong questions graciously.

In each of these instances, the Bible does not depict that the pray-ers' questions went unanswered. Jesus didn't ignore the disciples. He didn't even seem bothered by their incorrect questions. Instead, He was graciously attentive to them. He took their questions seriously.

The reality is that what you are asking for might be wrong. You might know that going into prayer. You may have even asked yourself prior to praying, "Should I pray this?" "I'm not sure I should pray for this." "Can I pray for this?"

Asking who is the greatest is not humble. Asking for your children to sit at Jesus' right and left in His kingdom is not humble. But in each instance these people were receptive to

Jesus' answer, which responded to something different from their original question.

That is humility.

Humble prayer accepts and embraces that what you are praying for might be wrong. Humble prayer also listens for God's response, which might address something altogether different from the original question.

Prideful prayer thinks words are the most important thing. People who pray pridefully only want an answer to their question. Prideful prayer never entertains the idea that God might be able to get past their words and listen to their heart.

In prayer, God is not so concerned with the words that you pray; rather, what He is really interested in is your heart. Instead of asking yourself, "Is what I'm praying wrong?" I'd prefer you to examine the kind of heart you have when you pray.

If your heart is humble, then I want you to pray—even for wrong things.

Not because I love when Christians pray for wrong things, but because I trust that God is able to listen to your prayer and respond with exactly what you need.

But if you simply refrain from praying because you're afraid you'll pray for the wrong thing, you've basically said your prayer is *so* wrong, *so* out of bounds, that not even an omniscient God could answer it.

You must be pretty incredible to outwit an omniscient God with your bad prayers.

What if that is exactly where Satan wants you? His desire is to discourage you from praying.

He does not want God involved. And what better way to do that than by simply getting in your head (and heart) that what you are asking for is wrong, so you shouldn't pray because surely God won't answer.

I can assure you that I know when I'm praying for something with the intention of manipulating God so that I can get what I want. It's not something to be proud of, but it's true.

Our hearts can deceive us into thinking we can do stuff like that.

However, even in those instances, because it is a desire of my heart, I still pray. Because just like the clay in the potter's hand, through persistent prayer, God begins to change my heart and reveal what it might look like to pray in a way that honors Christ. God has the amazing ability to create a humble heart even through prayer that starts out prideful.

God can handle a wrong prayer. His grace is able to withstand when one of His children prays for the wrong thing.

Sometimes when I suspect that what I'm asking for or about is wrong, I'll even preface my prayer with something like:

> Lord, you know my heart. You know everything about it. If what I'm asking for is wrong, please know that is not my intention. I just don't know how else to pray for it at the moment. I don't want to wait until I have the correct words to pray. I need You now. Please teach me, Holy Spirit, how to pray for this. Please convict me if what I'm asking for is wrong so that I might confess that sin.

Then I pray with whatever words I have available.

There is often a wide gap between my heart and the words I pray. It's as though my heart wants to express something to God, but I don't have all the words yet to verbalize it. So what ends up coming out is wrong, even though that wasn't my intention at all.

Looking back at my relationship with God, it has been those moments—sacred moments, really—when God has graciously given me the space to ask *wrongly* that I've learned to ask *correctly*. That kind of conversation with God only grows and matures if you are able to humbly endure the wrong moments in prayer.

CHAPTER 30

WE'RE GOING ON
A BEAR HUNT

It is always fun listening to Lolly and the kids talk in the car. Sometimes they have the goofiest conversations. Other times, they talk about serious topics. And I'm always amazed at how much a five- and three-year-old can comprehend.

Then there are those special moments when the kids don't even know how cute they are. Lolly will be talking about something somewhat serious, and one of the kids will say something in response and have no idea how funny it was.

One thing Lolly likes to do with the kids is to make a list of things—this could include objects or animals—and when someone finds it, they can check it off the list. One time when we were in the mountains, Lolly made a list of various animals to find in the woods.

Weeks later, on our way home from a birthday party, Lolly asked the kids a question:

Lolly: What are some ways you have experienced God, where you know He's there even if you can't see Him?

Kaden: I'm not really sure. I can't think of anything.

Oliver: Yeah, me neither.

Lolly: Remember that time in the mountains when we made a huge, long list of God's creation that we wanted to see, and in one day He showed us a bunch of His creation that we could check off our list? Wasn't that so cool the way God loved us and showed us His creation?

Kaden: Yeah, that was awesome!

Oliver: YEAH, awesome!

Lolly: God loves to hear your voice and hear your prayers, big or small. You can ask Him anything.

[The car is quiet.]

Kaden: *(whispering)* Dear God, please put an ice-cream cone in my hand right now.

Oliver: Yeah, ice cream, please!

God answers our prayers, but He is not a magic wizard. The boys didn't get any ice cream that day.

The reality is that if you pray long enough, you will encounter moments when you ask for something and never get a response. Ever. It will truly be an unanswered prayer.

When I first sat down to write this part of the book, I was anxious. At first, I wondered what I could say. In an earlier draft I had a chapter titled "Unanswered Prayer," and all I wrote was: "Sometimes God says no."

I wanted the reader to laugh a little, but also sit with that simple reality.

But as I kept writing and thinking and wondering, it became more and more evident that we claim a lot of prayer as unanswered prematurely—perhaps because God has exceeded our time frame or God didn't answer our prayer exactly how we envisioned it. We've already covered some of these things in the previous chapters.

But if you are going to talk about prayer, and particularly the humility desired by God in prayer, you have to include unanswered prayer.

It's essential.

Unanswered prayer might require more faith and humility than any other prayer. Why? You have to trust God in order to believe that He has not answered your prayer for good reason. For His reason. For His purpose.

And I'm not talking about coming to terms with God not placing an ice-cream cone in your hand. Rather, it's those moments when you pray for healing and God doesn't answer. This hurts a lot.

You pray for God to heal someone you love from cancer.

You pray for God to heal someone's broken marriage.

You pray for God to heal someone with an addiction that is causing so much harm to themselves and maybe even you.

"God, why won't You answer this prayer? Do You not care about this person? Out of all the prayers I pray, this seems like one You'd want to answer."

And yet there's nothing. Someone dies. Someone gets a divorce. Someone overdoses.

Faith says: *God is good even when I can't feel His goodness.*

This works in unanswered prayer too.

Faith says: *God is good even when the answer is no.*

That might be easy to read and comprehend, but to live with this subtle truth is profoundly difficult when it matters most. Let's talk more about this for a moment.

What I'm about to say doesn't solve the dilemma of unanswered prayer. I'm not sure that's even possible; that would require the mind of God. What we can do, though, is perhaps dispel the myth that God doesn't care. Because He does care, even when it might seem like He doesn't because your prayer was not answered.

Remember way back to the first few chapters when we talked about the idea of being naked (chapter 2) and clothed (chapter 3)? Remember how one of the important elements

> Faith says, *God is good even when the answer is no.*

of prayer was understanding that we partake in prayer as sinners?

This explains a lot of why it can feel awkward at times when we pray. It also explains why it feels like we are deficient in the words we can pray to God. Why we often feel like there is so much more to say, but we don't have the words yet.

That's also why I begged you not to wait for the correct words—just pray, even groan. God understands it all because He completely knows your heart.

Okay, but what does this have to do with unanswered prayer?

One of the sad realities about sin is that it has to run its course. After the Fall, sin entered the world, Adam and Eve became aware that they were naked, and they tried to clothe themselves with leaves (Gen. 3).

Sin and sin nature now must run its course, which means death has to run its course. Physical abnormalities have to run their course. Mental illness has to run its course.

But in the garden, just before Adam and Eve leave, God clothes them. God extends grace to them. Remember, God doesn't fix the problem. The problem has to run its course. But He extends grace nonetheless.

Later in the Bible God clothed us again—this time, with Himself through Jesus.

Then in the new heaven and the new earth, God clothes us again, with a glorified body. This body will be free from sin and all the abnormalities caused by sin.

This means there is no more death, divorce, addiction, pain, tears, and sadness.

Even though sin has to run its course, thankfully, God has a plan to defeat it. But it will take time.

And because no one knows when Jesus will return, it may take a long time. Remember, God isn't rushed in bringing about His plan.

So when you pray for someone you love to be healed from cancer, can God heal them right then and there? Of course, He can. And He might! When praying for someone with cancer, I always pray for God's healing, either through the doctors and medications, or through God's healing hand. Either way, I want to give God the glory.

But many times, people aren't healed. I don't know why sometimes people are healed and other times they aren't. However, what I do know is that until Jesus returns, we are living in a world in which sin has to run its course—which means not everyone will be healed in response to our prayers.

In the Gospels, when Jesus entered a city or town, the Bible never says He healed everyone of everything. He might've healed people from blindness, but that didn't mean they wouldn't throw their back out or hurt their knee.

When Lazarus, one of Jesus' close friends, died, the Bible says, "Jesus wept!" (John 11:35). Then Jesus raised him from the dead, which is so cool. But is it that cool? As a display of the lordship of Jesus even over death, yes! But the reality is that Lazarus had already died once, and now he would have to die again!

One of the sad truths about this reality is that death has to run its course. In other words, in this world, it is more natural for people to die than to be healed.

It's the same line of spiritual reasoning with divorce. How many kids, parents, and spouses have prayed for a divorce not to happen? Yet the divorce goes through. The marriage ends.

But doesn't God hate divorce? He does (Mal. 2:16 MSG).

However, sin has to run its course, which means when you have two sinners married to one another, for a host of reasons it can be really difficult for them to stay together. There are even biblical and theological reasons people might have to get divorced.

Next time you pray for a couple not to get a divorce, remember that God also desires to comfort you through this trial and testing of your faith. However, God is not going to override the individuals involved and force them to remain married.

In a sense, unanswered prayer is linked to sinfulness and sinful behavior. As long as sin is in the world, we can expect for unanswered prayer to persist. However, God's strength in times of unanswered prayer is found in the comfort only He can provide.

Trouble is, we think that strength is found in the answer to our prayer, but God wants to comfort us through the trial and testing of our faith.

Jesus experienced unanswered prayer too.

In the Gospel of Matthew, right after the Passover meal, Jesus and the disciples traveled to a garden called Gethsemane. Once there, Jesus took Peter, James, and John with Him to pray, and He told the three disciples, "I am deeply grieved, to the point of death. Remain here and stay awake with me" (Matt. 26:37–38).

> We think that strength is found in the answer to our prayer, but God wants to comfort us through the trial and testing of our faith.

Jesus was so filled with agony at the thought of the events to follow that He began to sweat drops of blood that dripped to the ground (Luke 22:44). Then He went off a little further and fell on His face and prayed.

For Jesus, in this moment of deep despair and sorrow, His first response was to pray.

His prayer wasn't for the sorrow and pain to go away. It was: "My Father, if it is possible, let this cup pass from me. Yet not as I will, but as you will" (Matt. 26:39).

The cup that Jesus was talking about is the cup of the cross. It is the blood that He was about to pour out on the cross for the forgiveness of sins (vv. 27–28).

While submitting to the Father, Jesus asked for another possible way. After He prayed, Jesus returned to find the disciples sleeping, and He said to Peter, "So, couldn't you not stay awake with me one hour?" (v. 40). Then He asked Peter to stay awake and pray.

"Again, a second time, he went away and prayed, 'My Father, if this cannot pass unless I drink it, your will be done'" (v. 42). And just like the last time, Jesus returned to find His disciples sleeping.

Then a third time, Jesus went away, and the Bible simply says that Jesus prayed the same thing, "saying the same thing once more" (v. 44).

Shortly after praying in Gethsemane, what Jesus foretold would happen did, in fact, take place. Judas returned in order to betray Jesus and hand Him over to the authorities (vv. 47–50).

Sometimes in our darkest moments—in our moments of sorrow and despair—it can feel isolating. It can feel as though we are all alone.

Even though Jesus had His disciples with Him, it didn't make what He was about to enter into any easier. The cross for Jesus was a lonely, isolated, painful event.

Was it wrong for Jesus to persistently pray for this cup to pass Him? Not at all. In fact, Jesus prayed more persistently as He felt more and more agony (Luke 22:44).

He prayed the same prayer three times, and unlike the widow from Luke 18, Jesus never received justice from His adversary. What's amazing, though, is that because the cup never passes, Christians receive true and ultimate justice against our adversary.

He becomes our justice through the pouring out of His blood on our behalf.

In addition, Jesus never received the three loaves of bread, like the friend in Luke 11. Instead, it is Jesus' body that would be broken and given to Christians—the bread of life.

Was Jesus wrongly praying for this cup to pass Him since He also knew it wasn't possible?

Was He asking the Father for something He knew the Father wouldn't answer?

It sure does look like that's the case.

It seems as though Jesus found comfort from the Father as He prayed for something He knew wouldn't be answered.

Luke 22:43 says that an angel from heaven appeared to Jesus while He was praying, giving strength to Him in time of need. But what Jesus did not receive was an explanation as to why the events to follow were going to take place. Jesus already knew this because He is God.

However, that did not exclude Him from the comfort and strength the angel provided.

What does that say about our own unanswered prayer? Could it be that Jesus modeled what our desires should be in times of unanswered prayer?

Yes, an answer would be helpful. And if our prayer cannot be answered, an explanation as to why our prayer will not be answered would be nice, right?

Yet Jesus didn't receive either of those in response to His prayer. He did receive help in the form of an angel who apparently gave Him the ministry of strength—strength to fulfill the Father's will.

Jesus' prayer was unanswered in that He didn't get what He asked for. Notice how Jesus asked for this cup to pass Him. In other words, if there was another way, Jesus would have liked to take that route. But there wasn't, and Jesus knew this.

Even though Jesus' prayer was unanswered, He did receive something: strength.

And boy, did He receive it.

Just finish the rest of Luke's Gospel, and watch in awe at Jesus' quiet, persistent, powerful strength to fulfill the Father's will.

Jesus had the strength to stand before Caiaphas, the high priest, and the scribes and elders—only to remain silent (Matt. 26:63). Then Jesus had the strength to stand before Pilate, and when He was accused, once again, He remained silent. Matthew writes: "But he [Jesus] didn't answer him on even one charge, so that the governor was quite amazed" (Matt. 27:14). Pilate was amazed at Jesus' strength.

Jesus had the strength to endure being mocked by the soldiers that were to lead Him away to be crucified. They stripped Him naked and put a scarlet robe on Him. They twisted together a crown of thorns and put it on His head (vv. 28–29). And the mockers said, "Hail, king of the Jews!" and they spit on Him (vv. 29–30).

Finally, Jesus had the strength to die on the cross, which was the most brutal and humiliating death one could imagine

(v. 50). The strength to offer Himself as the propitiation for our sins. And not for ours only, but for the whole world.

Jesus' prayer went unanswered; He didn't receive what He asked for. The cup would not pass over Him. However, He did receive strength in a real, tangible way.

One of my favorite books to read to Kaden and Oliver is *We're Going on a Bear Hunt* by Michael Rosen.[4] Our copy is old and weathered and has likely been read a hundred times.

The story begins with a family walking off into a field: "We're going on a bear hunt. We're going to catch a big one. What a beautiful day! We're not scared."[5]

As they go on their journey to find a bear, they come to all these impasses: "Oh-oh! A river! A deep, cold river. We can't go over it. We can't go under it. Oh, no! We've got to go through it!"[6]

Then it's: "Oh-oh! Mud! Thick, oozy mud. We can't go over it. We can't go under it. Oh, no! We've got to go through it!"[7]

I don't want to spoil the ending; you'll have to read it yourself.

But Rosen's book is one of the most profound theological treatises I've read on unanswered prayer.

Think of it this way: "Oh-oh! Cancer! Big, scary cancer. We can't go over it. We can't go under it. Oh, no! We've got to go through it!"

---

[4] Michael Rosen, *We're Going on a Bear Hunt* (New York: Little Simon, 1989).
[5] Ibid., 1.
[6] Ibid., 6
[7] Ibid., 10.

Or it's this: "Oh-oh! Divorce! Painful, icky divorce. We can't go over it. We can't go under it. Oh, no! We've got to go through it!"

The effects of the Fall make pain and suffering unavoidable—even with our best attempts, through prayer, to avoid the river or the mud by going over it, under it, and around it. The answer might be no. In order to get to the other side, you're going to have to go through whatever is before you.

Yet you never go through it alone as a Christian.

God gives you the strength to go through it. So while your prayer might go unanswered, it isn't as though you've been left behind. God will walk graciously with you, providing the strength to endure whatever obstacles might come your way.

If it is a rushing river, He'll clothe you. If it is thick mud, He'll clothe you. Divorce, death, or depression—He's with you.

CONCLUSION

BIG ANNOUNCEMENT!

Well, what do you think? Prayer isn't so intimidating, is it?

I hope not.

I hope that by now you're confident that you possess at this moment everything you need to begin praying. And not just begin praying, but to keep praying and never stop praying.

You've actually had it this whole time. It's your heart.

You do have a heart, right?

Since I started writing this book, a lot has happened in our family. I actually have a big announcement to make.

Lolly is pregnant!

Yep, here we go—three boys. I hope everyone enjoyed this book, because I won't have time to write another one for about fifteen years.

Kaden and Oliver are very excited to be big brothers. Oliver is especially excited that he gets to be a big brother and little brother at the same time.

It has been a tough season for many reasons, but one that has hit home for us is that, due to COVID-19, I haven't been able to go to one appointment with Lolly. I hadn't missed one with either boy before. Ever.

Recently, one of our friends let us borrow her Doppler heartbeat monitor so that we could hear our baby boy. We don't use it often, but every once in a while, we pull it out and check the baby's heartbeat with the boys so that they can hear what's going on in Mommy's belly.

Then we go to Kaden and Oliver and find their heartbeats too.

The last time we did this, Oliver really wanted to hear Daddy's heartbeat. So they put the machine up to my chest . . . and nothing.

Lolly couldn't find my heart! We looked all over my chest . . . and nothing.

Lolly said this explained a lot. Kaden followed her and said, "Yeah, Daddy, this explains a lot. I don't know what that means. But it explains a lot."

This would be the only scenario in which you couldn't pray. If we couldn't find your heart on the Doppler. Otherwise, you have all the necessary faculties to pray at this very moment.

I'm not sure if you ever thought of it like this, but prayer is a theological topic. Throughout this entire journey, you've spent all this time doing theology with me.

When talking about prayer, we are asking questions about God and seeking answers for how we might relate to Him in our fragile and finite language. It doesn't get more theological than that.

The greatest mistake we could have made was to separate life from theology, as though they don't belong together. The end result of theology shouldn't be information that sits in a book on a shelf at the library gathering dust. Theology should be intertwined with human experiences.

Theology comes alive when it intersects with life and over time influences and changes the way we live and pray. But change is never easy.

> Theology should be intertwined with human experiences.

That's why theology should make you laugh and cry. It is serious at times and can even make you mad. Theology brings joy and is hopeful. It helps you find comfort when nothing else can. It is often emotionally exhausting doing theology. But it is also necessary if we are going to learn about how someone should talk to God.

This book holds a theological secret, one that might very well change the direction of your life. The secret is that humility is the soul of true prayer. It's what He desires most. We've told this story in a lot of different ways, through a lot of different people, while always keeping our focus on God's greatest yearning.

I want to say thank you for going on this journey with me. That you are reading this page, after everything we've been through, means a lot. When someone lets you inform, and maybe even change a little, the way he or she thinks about God and talks to God, that is a sacred privilege.

I really do hope we meet again and that it isn't in fifteen years either.

Until then, may you prayerfully seek refuge in the name of the Lord a little more today than you did the day before. And if the Lord gives us tomorrow, then may you do this all over again. For that is a day, a week, a month, a year, a *life* well spent.